150 Delicious Dill Recipes

(150 Delicious Dill Recipes - Volume 1)

Erin Williams

Copyright: Published in the United States by Erin Williams/ © ERIN WILLIAMS

Published on December, 07 2020

All rights reserved. No part of this publication may be reproduced, stored in retrieval system, copied in any form or by any means, electronic, mechanical, photocopying, recording or otherwise transmitted without written permission from the publisher. Please do not participate in or encourage piracy of this material in any way. You must not circulate this book in any format. ERIN WILLIAMS does not control or direct users' actions and is not responsible for the information or content shared, harm and/or actions of the book readers.

In accordance with the U.S. Copyright Act of 1976, the scanning, uploading and electronic sharing of any part of this book without the permission of the publisher constitute unlawful piracy and theft of the author's intellectual property. If you would like to use material from the book (other than just simply for reviewing the book), prior permission must be obtained by contacting the author at author@sauterecipes.com

Thank you for your support of the author's rights.

Content

150 AWESOME DILL RECIPES 6

1. Hearty Salad From Your Fridge And Pantry 6
2. Very Simple Salmon Chowder 6
3. "Shrimp Evening" Dumplings 7
4. A Dilly Of A Chopped Salad 8
5. Adam's Chicken Pot Pie 8
6. Always Requested Roasted Potato Salad 9
7. Apple Stick And Dill Salad 9
8. Aromatic Poached Salmon With Rye And Caper Breadcrumbs 10
9. Avocado Asparagus Toast 10
10. Avocado Boats With Crab And Smoked Salmon 11
11. BRAISED CHICKEN WITH ASPARAGUS, PEAS, AND MELTED LEEKS 11
12. Bacon Cheeseburger Pizza With Dill Pickle Aioli 12
13. Bagel And Cream Cheese Strata 13
14. Baked Mushroom Rice Pilaf 3 Ways 13
15. Baked Salmon With Duchess Potatoes 14
16. Balkan Potato, Paprika And Green Bean Stew 14
17. Bay Scallops, Shrimp And Calamari Gratin, Flavored With Mortadella 15
18. Beet & Carrot Fritters With Dill & Yogurt Sauce 16
19. Blini With Crème Fraîche And Smoked Salmon 16
20. Breakfast Three Cheeses Stuffed Pita French Toast 16
21. Buttered Dilly Green Beans 17
22. Carrot Ginger Pancakes 17
23. Carrot Soup With Ramp Chips 18
24. Chicken "Stoup" 18
25. Chicken Gyro & Dill Ranch Sauce 19
26. Chunky Chilled Beet Borscht 20
27. Cider Braised Red Cabbage With Leeks .. 20
28. Citrus Salad With Shaved Fennel, Celery, And Cilantro Yogurt Dressing 21
29. Cold Salmon & Potatoes With Dill Yogurt & Paprika Oil 22
30. Cool Cucumber Soup With Persian Flavors 22
31. Corn Chowder With Smoked Salmon And Dill 23
32. Crab Cake Melt 23
33. Creamy Cucumber Salad With Yogurt And Spice 24
34. Creamy Dilled Green Bean Salad 24
35. Cucumber Salad 24
36. Dad's Favourite Baked Fish 25
37. Delicious Cabbage Pie 25
38. Dill Cucumber Salad With Shaved Machego 26
39. Dill Pickle Soup 26
40. Dill And Fennel Frond Potato Salad 27
41. Dill And Pea Pilaf 27
42. Dill(icious), Pickled Cucumber And Potato Summer Salad 27
43. Dilled Zucchini Soup For All Seasons 28
44. Eggplant Pide (or Eggplant Boats) 29
45. End Of Season Tomato Salad 29
46. Fish Cakes 30
47. Fraiche Start Carrot Quiche 30
48. French Lentil And Arugula Salad With Herbed Cashew Cheese 31
49. Fresh Dill Vegetable Dip 32
50. Fresh Tomato Sandwich 32
51. Gatsby's Harlequin Salad 33
52. Gena Hamshaw's (Vegan) Deli Bowls With Smashed Chickpea Salad 33
53. Goats Cheese & Aubergine Quinoa Oat Crust Pizza 34
54. Greek Lemon Soup —Avgolemono 35
55. Greek Yogurt Potato Salad 35
56. Grilled Calf's Or Beef Liver Served With A Famous Romanian Sauce Mujdei 36
57. Grilled Portabello Gyros 37
58. Grilled Stuffed Portabello Mushroom Burgers 37
59. Habanero Dill Pickles 38
60. Herring Salad 38
61. Homemade Labneh 39
62. Horseradish Hummus 39
63. Hungarian Creamed Zucchini (Anyu's Tök Főzelék) 40
64. Jane Grigson's Celery Soup 40
65. Jazzed Up Peas, Lemon And Pearl Onions

66. Kale Salad With Buttermilk Anchovy Dressing 41
67. Kale And Red Lettuce Salad W/ Goat Cheese, Pickled Cherries And Grilled Chicken .. 42
68. Kosher Pickles 42
69. Lamb Dolmas (Stuffed Grape Leaves) 43
70. Lamb Stuffed Peppers 44
71. Latke And Smoked Salmon Stacks 44
72. Lemon Thyme Grilled Fish With Cucumbers And Arugula 45
73. Lentil And Vegetable Soup 46
74. Light As Air Chickpea And Zucchini Fritters ~ Lemon, Herbs And Yogurt 46
75. Low Fat & Healthy Red Potato Salad 47
76. Middle Eastern Zucchini Fritters 47
77. Mild Cured Cucumbers 48
78. Mom's Mushroom Barley Soup 48
79. Moroccan Squash With Vegetable Almond Pilaf 49
80. Mushroom Stuffed Draniki 50
81. My Classic Burger With Special Sauce 50
82. New England Seafood Chowder 51
83. New Potato Salad With Crispy Radishes, Fennel & Celery 52
84. No Mayo New Potato Salad With Lemon, Dill, And Chives 52
85. Pashteda (Mushroom Pie) 52
86. Pressure Cooker Corned Beef Brisket With Charred Cabbage And Dill Vinaigrette 53
87. Purple Carrot Meze (Tarator) 54
88. Quick Pickles 54
89. Quinoa "Fried Rice" 55
90. Quinoa And Farro Salad With Pickled Fennel 55
91. Radish & Cucumber Salad 56
92. Radish Canapés 56
93. Rainbow Gazpacho 57
94. Rassolnik, Traditional Russian Soup With Pickles 58
95. Red Chard With Festive Spices 58
96. Red, White, And Blue Flannel Hash 59
97. Rice, Dill And Olive Filled Tomatoes 59
98. Roast Carrots With A Few Pals 60
99. Roasted Asparagus Soup With Lovage & Dill 60
100. Roasted Cauliflower Buttermilk Soup 61
101. Romanian Creamed Chicken (Ciulama De Pui) 61
102. Rounds, Roots And Shoots: A Vernal Salad 62
103. Salmon Soup With Mushrooms, Broccoli, Spinach And Corn 63
104. Salt And Vinegar Potato Salad {vegan} 63
105. Sardine Tartine 64
106. Schnitzel With German Cucumber Salad .. 64
107. Seafood, Fennel And Lime Salad 65
108. Seafood, Fennel, And Lime Salad 65
109. Seared Salmon With Herbal Lemon Emulsion 66
110. Smoked Salmon Couscous {with Feta And Dill} 66
111. Smoked Salmon Pate 67
112. Smoked Salmon And Pearl Cous Cous Salad 67
113. Smoked Trout Spread 68
114. Smoked Trout, Beet & Apple Salad With Trout Grebenes 68
115. Smoked Salmon Pasta 68
116. Spanakopita Frittata 69
117. Spanakopita Grilled Cheese 69
118. Spinach Crepes With Smoked Salmon And Lemony Greek Yogurt Sauce 70
119. Spinach Pie (spanakopita) 70
120. Spring's Beauty In A Bowl: A Simple Six Piece Salad 71
121. Squash Soup 72
122. Sticky, Spicy, Sweet Roasted Carrots And Chickpeas With Date Vinaigrette 72
123. Stovetop Smoked Sturgeon A La Russe 73
124. Stuffed Bell Peppers 74
125. Stuffed Grape Leaves & Tzatziki Sauce 75
126. Stuffed Mussels Mussels Dolmas 76
127. Summer Harvest Soup With Chilled Dill Yogurt 76
128. Superiority Burger's BBQ Baked Gigante Beans With Polenta & Coleslaw 77
129. Sweet And Spicy Quick Pickled Veggies ... 78
130. Tangy Creamy Buttermilk Cucumbers 78
131. The American Black Forest 79
132. Toasted Farro Salad With Roasted Leeks And Root Vegetables 79
133. Topinambour Soup With Black Trumpets 80
134. Traditional Sweet And Savory Finnish

Christmas Pastries "Joulutortut" 80
135. Tsukune "Matzah Ball" Soup 81
136. Turkish Style Red Lentil Soup With Purple Carrots 82
137. Twice Baked Smoked Salmon Mashed Potatoes 82
138. Vegan Mushroom Stew 83
139. Walnut Crusted Halibut 83
140. Warm Bread Salad With Smoked Salmon, Roasted Vegetables & Creamy Dill Dressing 84
141. Warm Lentil Salad With Goats Cheese, Cherry Tomatoes And Walnuts 85
142. Whisky Cured Salmon 85
143. Whole Wheat Crusted Chicken Pot Pie With Kale, Butternut Squash, And Fresh Herbs 86
144. Yellow Split Pea Soup With Dill & Edamame 87
145. Yemenite Chicken Soup 88
146. Zesty Cucumber Yogurt Dip 89
147. Zucchini Cupcakes With Lemon Dill Frosting 89
148. Zucchini Soup With Feta And Fresh Dill. 90
149. Beet Leaf Bundles 90
150. Tomates Farcies: Vegetarian & Beef Stuffed Tomatoes, Bonus QUINOA Salad 92

INDEX 94
CONCLUSION 97

150 Awesome Dill Recipes

***

1. Hearty Salad From Your Fridge And Pantry

Serving: Serves 4-6 | Prep: | Cook: |Ready in:

Ingredients

- • 2 cups rice fresh cooked or leftover
- • 1 tablespoon canola oil
- • 1 lemon or lime juiced
- • Zest of 1 lemon
- • 1 teaspoon salt
- • ½ teaspoons freshly ground black pepper
- • 4-5 chopped scallions
- • ½ cup mayonnaise
- • 1 can (15 ounces) pink salmon, drained, flaked and chilled
- • 1 thinly sliced celery rib with the lives
- • 1 tablespoon chopped dill or parsley
- • ½ cup petted olives halved

Direction

- Toss the rice with oil to coat and separate them. If fresh cooked, cool for about 1 hour.
- In a salad bowl mix lemon juice, salt, black pepper, scallions (leave about a tablespoon of the green part for garnish), celery, mayonnaise and olives.
- Gently mix-in the rice, half of the salmon, dill and lemon zest.
- Spoon to a platter or a nice shallow salad bowl.
- In the center arrange the remaining salmon.
- Garnish with lemon wedges or rounds, and sprinkle with the reserved green part of the scallions.

2. Very Simple Salmon Chowder

Serving: Makes 3 to 4 quarts | Prep: | Cook: |Ready in:

Ingredients

- 6 tablespoons butter, divided
- 2 large fat leeks, white and light green parts only
- 4 cups peeled potatoes cut into a 3/4 inch dice (I used 3 large redskins)
- 3 tablespoons flour
- 4 cups clam juice or fish stock
- 2 cups half and half
- 1 1/2 pounds boneless, skinless salmon cut in one inch cubes
- 1 cup minced fresh dill
- Salt and white pepper to taste

Direction

- Cut the leeks lengthwise into four quarters and then crosswise into 1/4 inch pieces.
- Melt 3 tablespoons of the butter in a good size soup pot and gently saute the leeks over medium heat until soft. Stir in the potatoes and flour and continue to saute to let the flour cook a little for about a minute.
- Add the fish stock or clam juice, bring up to a boil and then simmer the potatoes for about ten minutes until fork tender.
- Add the half and half and the fish. Bring barely up to a simmer (don't boil) for about 5 minutes. Stir in the remaining 3 tablespoons butter and the minced dill. Season with the salt and white pepper.

3. "Shrimp Evening" Dumplings

Serving: Makes 14-16 dumplings | Prep: | Cook: |Ready in:

Ingredients

- Shrimp Dumplings
- 2/3 cup warm water (about 110F)
- 1/4 teaspoon active dry yeast
- 2 cups all purpose flour
- 1 teaspoon sugar
- 1 teaspoon salt
- 1 pound shrimp, shells and tails removed
- dry white wine
- a large sprig of dill
- salt
- Mayonnaise and dill oil
- 1 cup fresh dill
- 1 1/2 cups olive oil, canola oil, or other oil (for the dill oil)
- 1 large egg yolk, at room temperature
- 2 teaspoons lemon juice (or pureed and strained unripe strawberry if you want to go very new Nordic)
- 1 teaspoon mustard
- 1/4 teaspoon salt
- 1 teaspoon cold water
- 3/4 cup neutral flavored oil such as canola or safflower (for the mayo)

Direction

- Shrimp Dumplings
- In a mixing bowl, combine the warm water, yeast, and sugar. Let stand until the yeast foams, about 5 minutes. Stir in the salt and enough of the flour to make a barely sticky dough.
- Knead the dough using just enough flour to keep it from sticking until it is supple and smooth, about 5-8 minutes (this can also be done in a mixer with a dough hook attached).
- Place in an oiled bowl, cover with plastic wrap or a damp towel and let rise somewhere warm until doubled in size, 1-2 hours.
- Meanwhile, place the shrimp and dill sprig in another bowl. Toss with a little sprinkling of salt, then add enough white wine to cover the shrimp. Refrigerate for 30 minutes to an hour. Then, drain off the wine and discard the dill.
- Chop the shrimp in a food processor until they are coarsely chopped.
- When ready to form the dumplings, divide the dough into 14-16 equal pieces. Roll each piece into a circle and place a spoonful of filling into the center of the circle. Use your palm and fingers to close up the dough around the filling, sealing it tightly. Repeat to form all the dumplings. (If you have leftover ground shrimp, you can fry it into tasty little patties, which make good snacks.)
- To cook the dumplings, either steam them in a steamer for about 8 minutes, or heat your oven to 425F, brush the dumplings lightly with an egg white and bake for 8-10 minutes, until they are baked through and they sound hollow-ish when tapped on the bottoms.
- Serve with homemade mayo and dill oil (see below).
- Mayonnaise and dill oil
- To make the dill oil: In a strainer, run super-hot water over the dill for about 1 minute, then dry. Coarsely chop the dill and transfer it to a blender. Pour in ½ cup oil and blend for 1 minute. Add the rest of the oil and blend for 2 minutes. Transfer to a covered jar and let rest for 24 hours, then strain.
- To make the mayo: In a medium bowl, whisk together the egg yolk, lemon juice, mustard, salt and 1 teaspoon cold water. Whisking constantly and vigorously, slowly dribble in the oil only a drop or two at a time until mayonnaise is thick and the oil is incorporated. When the mayonnaise has emulsified and is starting to get thick, you can add the oil in a thin stream. Continue until all the oil is added and the mixture has thickened to mayonnaise consistency.
- To serve: place a dumpling in the middle of a plate. Using a spoon, smear mayonnaise around it in 3/4s of a circle. Use a spoon or a squirt bottle to drizzle the dill oil around in a

3/4s circle mingling it with the mayo. Garnish with a few little bits of dill. Repeat to plate the remaining dumplings.

4. A Dilly Of A Chopped Salad

Serving: Makes 2 to 4 servings | Prep: 0hours0mins | Cook: 0hours0mins | Ready in:

Ingredients

- 1 cup sour cream
- 1/2 cup homeade or good quality mayo
- 1 clove garlic, mashed or pressed
- 1/2 cup fresh minced dill
- 2 tablespoons milk
- 6 slices crisp cooked bacon, reserving a tablespoon of the rendered bacon fat
- Salt, to taste
- 1/4 tablespoon black pepper
- 1 large heart of romaine lettuce, chopped
- 1/3 of an English cucumber, thinly sliced and then each slice halved
- 1/2 cup thinly sliced red onion, chopped
- 2 hard boiled eggs
- 3/4 cup crumbled blue cheese

Direction

- Combine the sour cream, mayo, fresh dill, salt, pepper and milk. Crumble 2 slices of the bacon very finely and add to the dressing along with the tablespoon of rendered bacon fat. Refrigerate until ready to serve.
- When ready to serve, combine the chopped lettuce, cucumbers and onions. Chop the bacon and eggs and add them to the mix. Gently fold in the blue cheese. Serve with the dilled bacon dressing.

5. Adam's Chicken Pot Pie

Serving: Serves 8 - 12 | Prep: 0hours0mins | Cook: 0hours0mins | Ready in:

Ingredients

- 1 bottle of cheap Sauvignon blanc
- 1 large onion, finely diced
- 2 teaspoons salt
- 3 cups milk, divided
- 1 - 3 cloves garlic, finely diced
- 1 teaspoon baking powder
- 8 tablespoons butter, divided
- 1 familly sized bag of mixed vegetables, frozen
- 1 teaspoon baking soda
- 6 tablespoons Crisco
- 1.5 pounds chicken meat, cut into 1 inch chunks
- 1/2 cup sharp cheddar, grated
- 4.5 cups all-purpose flour
- 2 tablespoons sugar
- 4 tablespoons dill weed
- 1.5 teaspoons savory
- 4 tablespoons olive oil
- 1 can Campbell's CCream of Chicken soup
- 4 tablespoons oil

Direction

- Pot Pie Stuff: Sauté the onion, garlic, and chicken in 2 tbsp. butter and 4 tbsp. oil. When the onions clarify and the chicken browns, lightly cover everything in the pot with 1/4 cup of flour. Stir well and immediately add enough wine to cover. Stir well.
- Pot Pie Stuff: Add the bag of frozen vegetables and continue stirring. Add 2 cups of milk, the soup, 2 tbsp. dill and 3/4 tsp of savory. If the mix is still gloppy, add a little more wine or milk until less so. Bring to a boil, then set on low heat to simmer for 10-15 minutes.
- Biscuit Crust: Sift 4 cups of flour into a large mixing bowl. Toss in sugar, baking powder, baking soda and salt. Cut in the Crisco, 6 tbsp. butter, and cheese with a ricer. Add remaining

2 tbsp. dill and continue cutting until dough resembles rice.
- Biscuit Crust: Add remaining 1 cup of milk; continue cutting dough until all the liquid is incorporated. Knead into a tight, lightly-damp ball.
- Bringing it Together: Pour the chicken pot pie stuff into a 12" round casserole dish. Pinch off 1" round pieces of dough, roll them in the palm of your hand, and squeeze into a disc. Starting at the edge and proceeding until you reach the middle, place the biscuit discs on the chicken.
- Bringing it Together: Dot the crust with butter or brush on an egg-wash: 2 egg yolks, a splash of milk & 2 splashes of wine, beaten well.
- Bringing it Together: Bake at 350 degrees Fahrenheit for 25 minutes or until the biscuits are golden-brown.

6. Always Requested Roasted Potato Salad

Serving: Serves 8 | Prep: | Cook: | Ready in:

Ingredients

- 2 pounds potatoes, yukon gold or other thin-skinned
- 2 tablespoons olive oil
- 1 teaspoon salt
- 1/2 cup low fat sour cream or yogurt
- 1/2 cup mayonnaise
- 1 teaspoon dijon mustard
- 1 teaspoon celery seeds
- 2 teaspoons celery salt
- 1 teaspoon white pepper
- 2 teaspoons seasoning salt
- 1/2 teaspoon sugar
- 1/2 cup sweet onions, finely chopped (soak onions in cold water to reduce bite if desired)
- 1 cup celery, finely chopped
- 4 tablespoons dill, chopped
- 1/4 cup cooked and chopped bacon, optional

Direction

- Preheat oven to 350 degrees. Wash potatoes and place in a baking dish. Put the oil over the potatoes, coating thoroughly. Bake for 45 minutes-1 hour until potatoes are tender but not mushy. Refrigerate until cool.
- Make the dressing: Add the sour cream, mayonnaise, mustard, all the seasonings, and the chopped vegetables. Stir thoroughly to blend and adjust seasoning to taste as necessary. Add the bacon if using. Refrigerate.
- When the potatoes are cool, remove the skins if desired by easily pulling them away from the potato. The skins can be left on; I usually leave on the skins of a few potatoes. Cut potato in half, then into batons, then into 1 inch chunks.
- Test seasoning on the dressing and adjust if necessary. Add the potato chunks and stir to mix thoroughly.
- Add the dill, mix, and serve!

7. Apple Stick And Dill Salad

Serving: Serves 6 | Prep: | Cook: | Ready in:

Ingredients

- 1/2 cup granulated sugar
- 1/2 cup apple cider vinegar
- 1 tablespoon chopped dill
- 3 tart apples cored and julienned
- 2/3 cup finely chopped onion
- 1/2 cup finely chopped dill pickle

Direction

- Combine sugar, vinegar and dill in a small bowl. Stir until sugar is dissolved.
- Mix the apples, onion, and dill pickle together and place in a medium size bowl. Add vinegar mixture and toss.
- Refrigerate until thoroughly chilled. At least one hour.

8. Aromatic Poached Salmon With Rye And Caper Breadcrumbs

Serving: Serves 4-6 | Prep: | Cook: | Ready in:

Ingredients

- Breadcrumbs
- 2-3 slices stale Pumpernickel dark rye, thick crusts removed (you want to end up with 1/2 cup of stale breadcrumbs)
- 2-3 slices stale French baguette, thick crusts removed (you want to end up with 1/2 cup of stale breadcrumbs
- Salmon
- 1/2 cup gin
- 1/2 cup water
- 1-1 1/2 pounds salmon fillet, preferably wild
- 3 tablespoons fresh Italian parsley, finely chopped
- 2 tablespoons fresh dill, finely chopped
- 2 tablespoons lemon zest
- 2 tablespoons unsalted butter
- 1 cup mixed Pumpernickel/French breadcrumbs (more crumb than sand)
- 1 1/2 tablespoons chopped capers
- 2 teaspoons prepared horseradish
- 1 tablespoon mayonnaise

Direction

- Breadcrumbs
- Note: Here in Hawaii, sliced bread molds faster than it gets stale. I sliced and cubed two pieces from each of my day old loaves and then popped them into a 350°F oven for about 10 minutes to dry out the bread a little more. Feel free to stale your bread using whatever technique works in your climate.
- Make your breadcrumbs by cubing your bread slices (Pumpernickel and French) and giving them a whirl in the food processor. Pulse until you have mostly uniform, smaller than pea-sized breadcrumbs (the bulk of the mix should be uniform; you'll also have pulverized sandy-looking bits). Be careful not to overheat your processor.
- Salmon
- In a sauté pan or skillet with a lid, add the gin and water. Place salmon in the center of your pan and evenly distribute parsley, dill and lemon zest on top of fish, pressing down slightly with your finger. Cover pan and bring to a simmer. Cook until desired doneness, about 6-7 minutes. Since you will be covering the fillet with breadcrumbs, it is okay to test doneness with a sharp knife in the center of fillet. Do not overcook. Transfer to a serving platter.
- While your salmon is poaching, get started on your breadcrumbs.
- In a skillet, melt the butter, and cook over medium heat, stirring occasionally until the butter begins to brown and is fragrant. Carefully add your breadcrumbs, and cook, stirring constantly until they are crisp and golden (the rye crumbs will be darker than golden), about a minute. Remove pan from heat and stir in capers, horseradish and mayonnaise. Thoroughly combine mixture using a heatproof spatula. Shower salmon with your breadcrumbs and enjoy!

9. Avocado Asparagus Toast

Serving: Serves 4 | Prep: | Cook: | Ready in:

Ingredients

- 4 slices whole grain bread, toasted
- 4 ripe avocados
- 1 bunch asparagus
- 1 handful fresh parsley, finely chopped (stalks also)
- 1 handful fresh dill, finely chopped (stalks also)
- 1 tablespoon extra virgin olive oil
- 4 tablespoons lime juice
- salt

- pepper
- 4 radishes
- 1 handful watercress

Direction

- Heat the water for blanching the asparagus. Salt your water well.
- Snap the ends of asparagus bending it until it naturally snaps. Wash and drain. Chop the tips off.
- When water boiling put the stalks into the pot and cook for 2-3 minutes, add the tips and cook for another minute.
- Remove from water, toss with olive oil and cool.
- Roughly chop the asparagus stalks. Save the tips to make your toast beautiful.
- Cut avocados in half, remove the pit, scoop the flesh into a bowl, add salt, pepper, 2 tablespoons lime juice, parsley and dill. Roughly mash everything together with a fork. Add chopped asparagus stalks and carefully combine with the mixture.
- In the meantime toast your bread.
- Spread avocado asparagus mash on your toast, toss the radish slices, watercress and asparagus tips on top of each toast. Drizzle with olive oil and rest of the lime juice.

10. Avocado Boats With Crab And Smoked Salmon

Serving: Makes 1 salmon and 1 crab boat | Prep: | Cook: | Ready in:

Ingredients

- Avocado Smoked Salmon Boat
- 1/2 avocado
- about 1/2 to 2/3 slice of mild smoked salmon
- 1 1/2 tablespoons creme fraiche
- 2 teaspoons chopped dill
- 2-3 teaspoons finely chopped shallots
- salt and pepper to taste
- Avocado Crab Boat
- 1/2 avocado
- about 1/4 cups lump crab meat, or to taste
- 1 teaspoon finely chopped cilantro
- 2 teaspoons very finely chopped red pepper
- 1 tablespoon very finely chopped cucumber
- salt and pepper to taste

Direction

- Avocado Smoked Salmon Boat
- Carefully scoop the avocado out of its peel with a spoon. Reserve the peel and cut the avocado into approximately 1/2 inch cubes.
- Chop the smoked salmon into about 1/2 inch squares. Mix it with the avocados and all other ingredients. Try to smush the avocado a little bit, but leave some chunks so it's not completely smooth. Add salt and pepper, more shallots or dill to taste.
- Scoop the dip back into the avocado peel. Garnish with a bit of creme fraiche and dill if desired. Serve with toast, chips or other crackers.
- Avocado Crab Boat
- Carefully scoop the avocado out of the peel with a spoon. Reserve the peel and chop the avocado into approximately 1/2 inch cubes.
- The red pepper and cucumber should be chopped into very small chunks, no larger than pea-sized. Carefully mix the avocado, crab, and the rest of the ingredients. The avocado should be partially smushed, but still chunky to compliment the crab bits.
- Add salt and pepper, and more red pepper, cucumber, or cilantro to taste. Scoop back into the avocado peel and garnish with cilantro if desired. Serve with toasts, chips, etc.

11. BRAISED CHICKEN WITH ASPARAGUS, PEAS, AND MELTED LEEKS

Serving: Serves 4 | Prep: | Cook: | Ready in:

Ingredients

- 2 medium leeks, white and light-green parts only, cut crosswise into 1/3-inch rounds
- 1/4 cup olive oil, divided
- 2 teaspoons kosher salt, divided
- 1/4 teaspoon reshly ground black pepper, plus more
- 2 teaspoons whole fennel seeds
- 8 bone-in chicken thighs (about 4 pounds)
- 1/2 cup Epicurious Chardonnay
- 1 1/2 cups low-sodium chicken broth
- 3/4 pound medium asparagus, trimmed, cut crosswise in half and on the bias
- 2 cups shelled fresh peas (from about 2 pounds pods) or frozen peas, thawed
- 1 tablespoon finely grated lemon zest
- 1/2 teaspoon finely grated lemon zest
- 2 teaspoons fresh lemon juice
- 3 tablespoons chopped dill

Direction

- If you see or feel dirt in the leeks, rinse well, separating layers, then pat dry; otherwise, leave rounds intact.
- Heat 2 Tbsp. oil in a large skillet over medium-high until hot but not smoking. Add leeks in a single layer; season with 1/4 tsp. salt and a pinch of pepper. Reduce heat to low and cook, turning once, until leeks are lightly golden, 16–18 minutes. Transfer leeks to a plate; reserve skillet.
- Lightly crush fennel seeds with the bottom of a heavy skillet or pot. Pat chicken thighs dry with paper towels and season with fennel, 1 1/2 tsp. salt, and 1/4 tsp. pepper. Heat remaining 2 Tbsp. oil in a 5–7-qt. Dutch oven or large wide saucepan over medium-high. Cook thighs, skin side down, until well-browned, 12–14 minutes. Transfer skin side up to a plate. Pour off and discard fat.
- Add Epicurious Chardonnay to pot, bring to a simmer, and cook, scraping up bits from bottom of pot, 1 minute. Add broth and return chicken skin side up to pot. Lower heat to medium-low, cover pot, and cook until chicken is cooked through, 15–18 minutes.
- Meanwhile, combine asparagus, peas, and 2 Tbsp. water in reserved skillet, cover, and cook over medium heat until asparagus is crisp-tender, about 5 minutes. Remove from heat. Add 1/2 tsp. lemon zest, remaining 1/4 tsp. salt, and a pinch of pepper; stir gently to just combine.
- Divide chicken, asparagus mixture, and reserved leeks among large shallow bowls. Bring broth to a simmer, add lemon juice, then ladle into bowls. Top with dill and remaining 1 Tbsp. lemon zest.

12. Bacon Cheeseburger Pizza With Dill Pickle Aioli

Serving: Makes 8 | Prep: | Cook: | Ready in:

Ingredients

- 1 pound store-bought or homemade pizza dough (I used Trader Joe's Whole Wheat Pizza Dough)
- 1/2 pound Groung Angus Beef
- 2 teaspoons Worecestershire Sauce
- 2 Slices of Bacon, Chopped Fine
- 1/2 cup Ketchup
- 2 tablespoons Tomato Paste
- 1/2 cup Sliced Onion
- 1 cup Shredded Cheddar
- 1 cup Shredded Mozzarella
- For the Aioli
- 1 tablespoon Fresh Dill, Chopped Fine
- 1 tablespoon Dill Pickle Juice
- 1/4 cup Mayo
- Toppings
- 1/2 cup Shredded Romaine Lettuce
- 1/2 cup Chopped Grape Tomatoes
- 1/2 cup Chopped Dill Pickles
- Shredded Romaine Lettuce for topping, about 1 cup

Direction

- Store-bought or homemade pizza dough (I used Trader Joe's Whole Wheat Pizza Dough)
- In a large skillet, brown the beef and chopped bacon together. Add the Worcestershire sauce and salt and pepper to taste.
- Roll out your pizza dough to fit your pizza stone, 12- 14 inches in diameter.
- Remove your pizza stone from preheated oven and carefully transfer the dough to the stone.
- To prepare the sauce, combine ketchup and tomato paste in a small bowl and stir to evenly combine.
- Spread the sauce evenly over the pizza dough and sprinkle on the beef and bacon mixture. Top with sliced onion, then the cheeses.
- Bake for 10-15 minutes or until cheese has melted and crust is golden brown.
- To make the aioli, whisk together mayo with chopped dill and pickle juice. Transfer to a ziplock or piping bag to drizzle over finished pizza.
- Remove pizza from oven and top with pickles, tomatoes and lettuce. Drizzle on desired amount aioli and serve on the side, if desired. Slice and serve.

13. Bagel And Cream Cheese Strata

Serving: Serves 8 | Prep: | Cook: | Ready in:

Ingredients

- 1 tablespoon butter
- 1 red onion, thinly sliced
- 5 cups cubed stale bagels
- 8 ounces thinly sliced lox or crumbled smoked salmon
- 2 tablespoons capers (optional)
- 2 tablespoons chopped dill (optional)
- 8 ounces cream cheese, cut into half-inch cubes (as much as it's possible to cut cream cheese into cubes)
- 8 large eggs
- 2 cups half and half
- 1 teaspoon each salt and ground pepper

Direction

- In a large sauté pan, heat the butter over medium-high heat until it is foaming. Add the red onion and cook until softened and starting to brown, about 5 to 7 minutes.
- Butter a large baking pan (9 x 13 or so) and layer the cubed bagels, the salmon or lox, the sautéed onions, the cream cheese pieces, and the capers and dill (if using) in the pan. In a large bowl whisk together the eggs with the half and half and the teaspoons of salt and pepper. Pour the egg mixture over the bagels, etc., in the baking pan. Cover and let this sit for at least 45 minutes (you can also let it sit in the fridge overnight).
- When ready to bake, heat your oven to 350° F. Bake the strata until the eggs are set, about 45 minutes to an hour. Allow to cool for about 10 to 15 minutes before cutting into it. Eat warm or at room temperature.

14. Baked Mushroom Rice Pilaf 3 Ways

Serving: Makes 4 to 6 servings | Prep: | Cook: | Ready in:

Ingredients

- 3 tablespoons butter
- 1 tablespoon olive oil
- 8 ounces sliced mushrooms (your choice)
- 3/4 cup minced onion
- 1/4 cup diced celery
- 1 cup raw, long grain rice
- 2 cups chicken broth, plus a little more if needed (depending on your oven)
- 1/2 teaspoon black pepper
- 2 tablespoons minced fresh dill
- Chopped parsley for garnish (optional)
- 2 - 3 handfuls of torn baby spinach leaves (optional)

- 1/4 cup crumbled feta cheese (optional)

Direction

- In a large sauté pan, sauté the mushrooms in the butter and oil over high heat, until the mushrooms brown.
- Lower the heat to medium and stir in the celery and onion, and sauté until the onion softens.
- Stir in the cup of rice and continue to cook for a minute or two.
- Add the broth, pepper and dill and transfer to a medium baking dish.
- Bake, covered for 30 minutes at 350F. After 30 minutes remove cover and continue to bake another 10 (at this point you might need to add a little more broth).
- Serve as is or garnished with the parsley...or stir in the spinach leaves and/or the feta.
- NOTE: I just realized with all the combinations available, it's pilaf more than 3 ways!

15. Baked Salmon With Duchess Potatoes

Serving: Serves 4 | Prep: | Cook: | Ready in:

Ingredients

- 4 Salmon filets, no thicker than about 1/2 inch thick
- 4 medium Russet potatoes, diced
- 1/3 cup half & half or whole milk
- 2 tablespoons butter
- 2-3 tablespoons freshly grated horseradish, or to your taste
- 1 1/2 teaspoons salt, plus more for the salmon
- 1/2 teaspoon white pepper, plus more for the salmon
- 1 egg, beaten
- olive oil for the pan
- 1 tablespoon fresh dill, chopped

Direction

- In a large pot, boil the potatoes for 15-20 minutes or until tender. Remove from heat, drain and return them to the pot.
- Mash the potatoes with a masher or potato ricer until smooth with no chunks.
- Add the half & half or milk, butter, horseradish, salt and pepper. Mix well and taste to adjust seasonings.
- Add the beaten egg and set aside.
- Preheat the oven to 425 degrees.
- Rinse the salmon and pat dry with a paper towel. Season with salt and white pepper.
- Oil a baking pan with olive oil. Place the salmon skin side down onto the pan.
- Spoon the potato mixture into a pastry bag with a large tip (or a make shift pastry bag made out of a plastic baggy).
- Pipe the potatoes onto each salmon filet in the pattern of your choice. I made rows of little stars. You could also just smooth the potatoes on the salmon with a spoon.
- Bake the salmon for 15-20 minutes or until the potatoes start to get golden.
- Sprinkle the fresh dill on top and serve.

16. Balkan Potato, Paprika And Green Bean Stew

Serving: Makes about 4 servings | Prep: | Cook: | Ready in:

Ingredients

- 2 tablespoons extra virgin olive oil
- 1 large leek (white and pale green part only), diced
- 8 large cloves garlic, halved
- 2 tablespoons sweet Hungarian paprika
- 1 teaspoon salt
- 1/2 teaspoon black pepper
- one 14.5 ounce can plum tomatoes crushed a bit with your clean hands
- 2 cups chicken or vegetable broth

- 3/4 of a pound of fresh young green beans, trimmed and halved
- 5 medium Yukon Gold or russet potatoes, peeled and quartered
- 1 tablespoon fresh minced dill plus more for garnish

Direction

- Heat the oil in a Dutch oven or soup pot, add the diced leek and sauté until softened. Add the garlic halves, salt, pepper and paprika and continue to sauté for a minute more.
- Stir in the tomatoes, broth and green beans, bring up to a boil and then down to a slow simmer and simmer, partially covered for about 30 minutes until the green beans are soft. Give everything a stir a couple of times while simmering.
- Add the potatoes, bring back up to a simmer and continue to simmer for about 20 minutes or until the potatoes are fork tender.
- Off the heat, stir in the tablespoon of dill. Serve in bowls, garnished with a few dill sprigs.

17. Bay Scallops, Shrimp And Calamari Gratin, Flavored With Mortadella

Serving: Serves 6 | Prep: | Cook: | Ready in:

Ingredients

- • 5 tablespoons unsalted butter, melted and divided
- • 4 large garlic cloves, chopped
- • 2 medium shallots, chopped
- • 4 ounces Italian-style Mortadella, chopped
- • 2 tablespoons fresh parsley+ 1 tablespoon fresh dill, chopped
- • Zest and juice of 1/2 large lemon
- • 2 teaspoons freshly grated on a microplane ginger
- • 4 tablespoons dry white wine, I used White Zinfandel
- • 1 teaspoon kosher salt
- • 1/4 teaspoon red pepper flakes
- • 4 tablespoons good olive oil
- • 3/4 cup Panko breadcrumbs
- • 1/2 pound of each; fresh small bay scallops, whole medium shrimp, shelled and deveined, calamari, cleaned, washed and cut in about 1/3-inch rings, everything pat dry with paper towels
- • Fresh parsley and dill for garnish

Direction

- Preheat the oven to 425 degrees F. Place a 9 or 10-inches gratin dish on a sheet pan; evenly spread 2 tablespoons of the melted butter in the bottom of the gratin dish.
- In a ball of a food processor combine garlic, shallots, Mortadella, herbs, lemon juice, ginger, wine, salt, red pepper flakes and olive oil. Pulls a few times until all the ingredients are evenly diced but not mushy; you should still be able to see each of the ingredients.
- Transfer to a mixing bowl; stir in lemon zest and reserve about 1/3 cup of this mixture; then fold in all the seafood, taste and add some more salt, if needed. Evenly spread in the bottom of the gratin dish. Mix the remaining 3 tablespoons of melted butter with Panko breadcrumbs; add reserved 1/3 cup of the Mortadella mixture. Spoon and evenly spread over the top.
- Place on the rack in the upper third of the oven; bake for 18 to 20 minutes, until the top is golden and sizzling and the seafood is barely done. If you want the top crustier, place the dish under the broiler for 2 minutes, until browned. Finish with a squeeze of fresh lemon juice and a sprinkling of parsley and dill; serve immediately with crusty bread.

18. Beet & Carrot Fritters With Dill & Yogurt Sauce

Serving: Serves 4 (makes 8 fritters) | Prep: 0hours30mins | Cook: 0hours30mins | Ready in:

Ingredients

- For the fritters:
- 2 1/2 tablespoons peanut oil
- 1 small onion, finely chopped
- 2 garlic cloves, crushed
- 1 large russet or Yukon gold potato
- 3 large carrots
- 2 large beets
- 2 eggs, lightly beaten
- Salt and black pepper
- For the sauce:
- 1 cup Greek yogurt
- 2 garlic cloves, crushed
- 1 tablespoon extra-virgin olive oil
- 1 tablespoon chopped dill leaves, plus extra to serve

Direction

- Heat 1/2 tablespoon of the peanut oil in a large nonstick skillet and gently sauté the onion until it is soft but not browned. Add the garlic and cook for another two minutes. Put into a bowl.
- Coarsely shred all the other vegetables, keeping them separate. After you finish shredding each type of vegetable, put them into a dish towel and squeeze out excess moisture. (Better use paper towels for the beets as they will really stain your dish towel.) Add the vegetables to the onion with the eggs, season well and mix together. Make the sauce by mixing all the ingredients together.
- Heat another 1 tablespoon of peanut oil in the skillet. Spoon enough mixture into the pan to make a batch of fritters each about 3 1/2 inches in diameter. Cook over a medium heat until a crust forms on one side, then carefully turn each over and cook on the other side again until a crust forms. Don't overbrown them or they will burn on the outside before they are cooked inside. After the crust forms, reduce the heat right down and cook for four to five minutes on each side, or until the vegetables are cooked through. (You'll know from the taste whether they are cooked right through. The potato becomes sweet.) You can keep the cooked fritters in a low oven while you finish the others, adding more oil to the pan to cook them if necessary.
- Serve the fritters with the yogurt sauce, sprinkled with more dill.

19. Blini With Crème Fraîche And Smoked Salmon

Serving: Makes 8-10 servings as an appetizer | Prep: | Cook: | Ready in:

Ingredients

- 1 recipe Buckwheat Blini (https://food52.com/recipes...)
- 2/3 cup creme fraiche
- 4 ounces smoked salmon
- 1/3 cup dill sprigs
- freshly ground black pepper

Direction

- Top each blini with 1 teaspoon crème fraiche. Divide the salmon evenly between the blini, on top of the crème fraiche.
- Top each with a sprig of dill and a grating of freshly ground pepper. Serve immediately.

20. Breakfast Three Cheeses Stuffed Pita French Toast

Serving: Makes 8 | Prep: | Cook: | Ready in:

Ingredients

- • 4 6 or 7-inches in diameter not too thick best quality pitas, cut in half
- • 1 cup fresh whole milk ricotta, homemade or prepared
- • 3/4 cup feta, Greek or French
- • 3/4 cup soft goat cheese
- • 2 tablespoons sour cream or crème fraîche
- • Green tops of 4-5 scallions or chives, chopped
- • 1 tablespoon fresh dill, parsley or cilantro leaves, chopped
- • 1/2 jalapeno pepper, seeds and membranes removed, diced
- • Coarse salt, if needed
- • Pinch of freshly ground black or white pepper
- • 2 large eggs, beaten with a splash or two of whey, milk or cream
- • Canola oil and unsalted butter for frying

Direction

- In a bowl of a food processor combine the cheeses and sour cream or crème fraîche; pulls a few times until uniform and smooth.
- Transfer to a mixing bowl and incorporate scallions, dill or any herb you like and diced jalapeno. Taste and add salt, if needed.
- Fill each half of pitas with about 2-2 1/2 full tablespoons of the cheese filling. Lightly press to evenly distribute and trying not to tear. Refrigerate until ready to serve.
- To serve; heat a frying pan on medium, add 1 tablespoon olive oil and 1/2 tablespoon butter spoon. In a shallow dish beat eggs and whey or whatever liquid you are using with a pinch of salt and pepper.
- Dip each side of the filled pitas, and fry for 2 to 3 minutes on each side or until golden brown. Quickly drain on paper towels, then orange on a serving platter or individually.
- Serve while steel hot with sour cream or crème fraîche or your favorite condiments or salads. Although the cheese filling is savory and even slightly spicy, I like mine with some jam or honey and roasted, lightly salted peanuts.

21. Buttered Dilly Green Beans

Serving: Serves 4 | Prep: | Cook: |Ready in:

Ingredients

- 2 cups (about a pound) of string beans, trimmed
- 1/2 teaspoon kosher salt
- 1-2 tablespoons chopped dill (more of less - depends how much you like dill)
- 2 tablespoons butter

Direction

- Bring a medium pot of water to a boil. Add the salt and return to a boil.
- Add the green beans and continue to boil on high for about two minutes until the beans look cooked but are still bright. Test one if you're not sure.
- Drain the beans in a colander. Quickly pour cold water over them to stop the cooking. Let them drain completely, for at least a few minutes.
- Meanwhile, melt the butter in a frying pan over medium-low heat. Add the green beans and cook for 2-3 minutes, stirring a few times, till the beans are warmed through and the butter is coating them evenly.
- Toss the string beans with the dill and serve.

22. Carrot Ginger Pancakes

Serving: Makes 12 | Prep: | Cook: |Ready in:

Ingredients

- 3 carrots, peeled and grated
- 1 clove garlic, peeled and grated
- 1 teaspoon freshly grated ginger
- 1 tablespoon fresh dill, finely chopped
- 1 egg
- 1/2 cup plain Greek yogurt

- 1/3 cup quinoa flour
- 1/2 teaspoon coriander
- 1/2 teaspoon turmeric
- 1 pinch salt
- 1 pinch freshly cracked black pepper
- 1 dash Sriracha
- 1 tablespoon butter, for greasing the griddle

Direction

- Take the grated carrot, garlic and ginger and squeeze them with a paper towel to get out the excess moisture. Combine them in a large bowl with the dill, egg, yogurt, quinoa flour, coriander, turmeric, salt, black pepper and Sriracha. Stir the mixture thoroughly until it is a uniform batter.
- Preheat an electric griddle to 350 or a griddle pan over medium high heat. Lightly grease it with the butter. Use a 1.5 inch cookie scoop to scoop perfect sized dollops of the batter onto the griddle. Flatten each of them gently with the back of the scoop into pancakes. Cook the pancakes for 2-3 minutes on each side in 2 batches of 6. This recipe yields 12 little pancakes using the 1.5 inch scoop measurement.
- Move the first batch to a plate when they are cooked and cover them with foil to keep them warm while the second batch cooks. When the pancakes are all done, serve them immediately as an amazing appetizer, light lunch or side dish! Enjoy!

23. Carrot Soup With Ramp Chips

Serving: Serves 6 to 8 | Prep: | Cook: | Ready in:

Ingredients

- 6 tablespoons vegetable oil
- 1/2 cup finely chopped onion
- 4 large carrots, peeled and chopped
- 1/8 teaspoon ground nutmeg
- salt
- 1/2 celery stalk, chopped
- 1 cup milk
- 5 large ramp bulbs, thinly sliced
- 1 tablespoon roughly chopped fresh dill
- freshly ground black pepper

Direction

- Warm 2 tablespoons of the oil in a large saucepan over medium-low heat. Add the onion, stir and cook until softened, about 5 minutes. Add the carrots, nutmeg and a large pinch of salt and cook for another five minutes, stirring occasionally. Then add the celery and cook for 3 more minutes.
- Add 3 cups of water, stir and increase the heat. Bring to a boil, cover and reduce the heat so that the soup is just simmering. Cook for about 25 minutes, until the vegetables are tender. Use a food processor to partially purée half the soup with 1/2 cup of the milk, keeping some texture. Put the other half of the soup in a blender with the rest of the milk and blend until completely smooth. If you prefer, you can pass the soup through a food mill or simply mash everything up with a spoon or a potato masher—you will end up with a chunkier soup, but it will still be delicious.
- When you're ready to eat, make the ramp chips. Heat the remaining 4 tablespoons oil in a small frying pan over medium-low heat and add the sliced ramps. Cook, stirring frequently, until the ramps are crispy and brown, about 3 minutes. Remove the chips with a slotted spoon and drain briefly on paper towels. Sprinkle lightly with salt.
- Stir the dill into the soup and reheat gently, adding more salt if necessary and some pepper. Serve the soup in warm bowls with a sprinkling of ramp chips on top.

24. Chicken "Stoup"

Serving: Serves 4 to 6 | Prep: | Cook: | Ready in:

Ingredients

- 2 lbs. chicken pieces, on the bone (dark meat is best, but you can use a mix if you'd like)
- 3 medium carrots, peeled
- 3 stalks celery
- 1 large sweet onion, peeled
- 2 cups homemade or good quality chicken stock
- Salt
- 2 tablespoons chopped fresh dill
- 1 lemon
- Freshly ground black pepper
- Crusty bread for serving

Direction

- Remove the fat from the chicken pieces, saving it if you like to make your own schmaltz or something. Put the chicken in a large soup pot. Cut one of the carrots into large chunks and add these to the pot with the chicken. Cut one stalk of celery and half the onion into similar sized chunks and add to the pot. Add the chicken stock and then enough water to submerge the chicken and vegetables. Add a generous pinch or two of salt. Bring to a boil over high heat and then lower the heat so that it simmers gently. During the first 5 minutes, skim any of the foam that accumulates on the surface with a shallow spoon. Cook the chicken for about 10 minutes, just until it's firm and opaque. Transfer to a plate, cover loosely with foil, and let the chicken cool for a few minutes while you continue to simmer the stock, partially covered.
- Remove the chicken from the bones and reserve the meat, returning the bones to the pot. Re-cover and simmer the stock for at least 45 minutes more. Remove the bones and the vegetables with a slotted spoon and discard, and then strain the stock through a fine mesh sieve into a clean pot.
- Cut the remaining carrots and celery into bite-sized chunks, and then do the same with the onion. Return the stock to a simmer and taste for seasoning, adding more salt if necessary. Add the carrots and onion to the pot and simmer for 5 minutes. Add the celery and cook for another 3 minutes, then stir in the dill, a good amount of lemon juice and several grindings of black pepper.
- When you're ready to serve the soup, tear or cut the chicken into bite-sized pieces and add it to the pot. Simmer for a minute or so, just until the chicken has a chance to reheat. (Be vigilant here -- this is the step that determines whether your chicken is tender or dry.) Taste once more for salt, and then serve immediately in shallow bowls with some good, crusty bread.

25. Chicken Gyro & Dill Ranch Sauce

Serving: Serves 6 | Prep: | Cook: | Ready in:

Ingredients

- Chicken Spice Rub
- 4 chicken breasts, cut in the center
- 1/4 teaspoon allspice
- 1/2 teaspoon garlic powder
- 1/2 teaspoon Mrs. Dash onion & herb
- 3/4 teaspoon cajun seasoning
- 1 teaspoon salt
- 1/2 teaspoon pepper
- 3 tablespoons olive oil
- 4-6 flat breads
- sliced tomatoes, lettuce, onions
- Creamy Dill Ranch Sauce
- 1 bunch fresh dill
- 2 garlic cloves
- 1/2 cucumber, peeled and cubed
- 3/4 cup sour cream
- 1/3 cup mayonnaise
- 2 tablespoons Parmesan cheese
- 3 tablespoons organic whole milk
- 1 tablespoon lemon juice
- 1 garlic clove
- 1 teaspoon salt
- 1/2 teaspoon pepper

Direction

- Chicken Spice Rub
- Mix all spices together in a small bowl.
- Add olive oil and mix well.
- Spread the rub all over the chicken breasts.
- Heat a large skillet over medium heat, and add about 2 tsp olive oil, then chicken.
- Cook until chicken is done, transfer to a plate to cool. Slice in strips for gyros.
- Creamy Dill Ranch Sauce
- Place dill, garlic, and cucumber in a food processor, and mix on high until finely chopped.
- Place in a medium mixing bowl, and add other ingredients mixing well.
- Use foil to wrap the gyro, having the foil cover half of the wrap. Place chicken down the center, and drizzle the sauce, then top with lettuce, tomato, and onions if desired. Roll up sealing the end with foil, and enjoy!

26. Chunky Chilled Beet Borscht

Serving: Serves 4 to 6 | Prep: | Cook: | Ready in:

Ingredients

- 1 tablespoon coconut oil (I prefer to use this for all heated applications)
- 1 yellow onion, diced
- 2 garlic cloves, minced
- 3 celery stalks, sliced
- 2 carrots, sliced into circles
- 15 - 20 baby red potatoes, halved or quartered as you prefer
- 4 medium-to-large sized beets, peeled and cut into 1/2 inch chunks
- 6 cups vegetable broth
- 1 1/2 cups cooked chickpeas
- juice of half a lemon
- 1/4 cup fresh dill, minced
- salt and pepper

Direction

- Heat the oil in a large soup pot over medium heat. Add the onions with a pinch of salt and sauté for about 5 minutes, till slightly browned and translucent. Turn the heat down to medium low and add the garlic; cook 30 seconds.
- Now, add the celery, carrots, and potatoes. Stir them around and cook for about 2 minutes. Then, add the beets along with the vegetable broth. If all the vegetables are not submerged, add a bit more broth.
- Turn the heat up to high and bring the soup to a boil. Once boiling, cover the soup, but leave the lid slightly ajar so that steam can escape. Turn the heat down to medium low and simmer for about 35 minutes, or until all the vegetables are tender.
- Add the cooked chickpeas, lemon juice, and dill. Stir into the soup. Taste for seasoning, adding lots of black pepper and however much salt you think the soup needs.
- Turn off the heat, and let the soup completely cool at room temperature. Transfer the soup to the fridge to chill for a few hours. Once it's nice and cold, serve!

27. Cider Braised Red Cabbage With Leeks

Serving: Serves 4-6 | Prep: | Cook: | Ready in:

Ingredients

- 3 tablespoons extra virgin olive oil
- 4 medium leeks, white and light green parts only, sliced
- 4 cloves of garlic, minced
- kosher salt and fresh ground black pepper, to taste
- 1 1/2 teaspoons dried thyme
- 1 small to medium red cabbage, cored and shredded
- 1 1/2 cups hard cider OR
- 1 cup vegetable or chicken stock AND

- 1/2 cup apple cider
- zest and juice of 1 lemon
- 3 tablespoons fresh dill, chopped

Direction

- Sauté the leeks, thyme and garlic in the olive oil, sprinkling with kosher salt to sweat, about 1-2 min.
- Add in the shredded cabbage and a generous amount of freshly ground pepper and sauté several minutes more just until the cabbage starts to wilt and its sugars begin to caramelize slightly.
- Add in the hard cider (or mixture of regular cider and broth), bring to a boil, then reduce and simmer for about 10 minutes or until almost all of the liquid has evaporated and you have a rather thick sauce. You want the cabbage to be moist but neither dripping in liquid, nor dry.
- Remove from the heat and add in the lemon zest, juice and dill, checking for seasoning and adding more salt and pepper if needed.
- This dish is great as a side dish alongside pork chops and some mashed turnips, or even on its own as a lunch.

28. Citrus Salad With Shaved Fennel, Celery, And Cilantro Yogurt Dressing

Serving: Serves 4 to 6 | Prep: | Cook: | Ready in:

Ingredients

- For the clantro-yogurt dressing:
- 1 teaspoon whole coriander seeds
- 1/2 teaspoon whole cumin seeds
- 1 tablespoon minced garlic
- 1 teaspoon finely minced ginger
- 1 teaspoon Ruby Red grapefruit zest, plus 2 tablespoons juice
- 1 pinch chile powder
- 1/2 cup Greek yogurt
- 3 tablespoons extra-virgin olive oil
- 1 tablespoon minced dill
- 1 tablespoon minced cilantro
- 1/4 teaspoon sea salt
- 1/4 teaspoon black pepper
- For the salad:
- 1 bulb fennel
- 6 stalks celery
- 1/2 shallot
- Sea salt, to taste
- 2 Ruby Red grapefruits
- 2 Cara Cara oranges
- 2 tablespoons cilantro leaves, plus more for garnish
- 1 tablespoon chopped dill, plus more for garnish
- 1 pinch ground coriander and cumin mixture
- 1/2 teaspoon black pepper

Direction

- Start with the dressing. Set a small sauté pan over medium heat. Add the coriander and cumin and toast, shaking once or twice, for about 45 seconds, just until spices have darkened just a shade or two and smell fragrant. Using a mortar and pestle or spice grinder, grind toasted seeds to a fine powder.
- In a small mixing bowl, use a fork to combine the garlic, ginger, and grapefruit zest and juice, 1 1/2 teaspoons of the ground coriander and cumin mixture (reserve any extra for garnishing later on), and a pinch of chile powder. Use the fork to slowly beat in the yogurt, followed by the olive oil. Stir in minced herbs, and add sea salt and pepper to taste.
- To prepare the salad, cut away any green fennel fronds and reserve for garnish. Cut the core out of the fennel and shave thinly on a mandoline. Trim the celery and shave at a diagonal into thin slices. Shave the shallot. Set shaved vegetables in a large bowl and sprinkle with a pinch or two of sea salt. Toss with a tablespoon of the yogurt dressing and set aside while you prepare the fruit.

- Cut off tops and bottoms of the citrus, cut off the peel and pith with a downward motion, and supreme the fruit.
- Fold the herbs into the shaved vegetables, and add several more tablespoons dressing. Adjust salt levels as needed. Arrange on a serving platter and tuck citrus wedges throughout. Garnish with any reserved fennel fronds, dill, and cilantro, plus a pinch each of the toasted spice mixture and black pepper.
- To best capture the fragrance and flavor, this salad is best enjoyed right away. If making ahead, you'll want to keep all the main elements separate until just before serving.

29. Cold Salmon & Potatoes With Dill Yogurt & Paprika Oil

Serving: Serves 2 to 3 | Prep: 6hours0mins | Cook: 0hours35mins | Ready in:

Ingredients

- Extra-virgin olive oil
- 12 ounces salmon fillet, skin removed
- Kosher salt
- 1 pound small yellow potatoes, halved or quartered
- 1 teaspoon smoked paprika
- 3/4 cup whole-milk Greek yogurt
- 1 cup roughly chopped dill, divided

Direction

- Heat the oven to 275°F. Sprinkle the salmon all over with salt. Drizzle olive oil on the bottom of a baking dish. Add the salmon and drizzle more on top. Roast for 15 to 25 minutes, flipping halfway through, until an instant-read thermometer reaches 120°F in the center. (If you don't have a thermometer, it should flake easily with a fork.) Let cool until just warm, then cover and transfer to the fridge until completely cold.
- Whenever you're ready to eat, cook the potatoes in salted boiling water (I estimate 1 tablespoon of kosher salt per quart of water) until knife-tender—start checking at 8 minutes, though it may take closer to 12.
- While those are cooking, heat 1/4 cup of olive oil in a tiny saucepan or skillet. As soon as it's hot, cut the heat and use a fork or mini-whisk to stir in 1 teaspoon paprika and a big pinch of salt.
- Blend the yogurt and 2/3 cup dill in a food processor, scraping down as needed, until the dill is completely incorporated and the yogurt is bright green. Season with salt to taste.
- Once the potatoes are done, drain them and sprinkle with salt. Let cool for a bit while you use a fork to break apart the salmon into flakes. Swoosh the dill yogurt on the bottom of the plates, then top with the flaked salmon and potatoes. Drizzle with some paprika oil and sprinkle with the remaining dill. Serve with the rest of the paprika oil to drizzle as you eat.

30. Cool Cucumber Soup With Persian Flavors

Serving: Serves 4 to 6 | Prep: | Cook: | Ready in:

Ingredients

- 1/4 cup golden raisins
- 4 small Persian cucumbers, diced
- 2 cloves of shallot, thinly sliced
- 1/2 teaspoon salt
- 3 cups yogurt
- 1/2 cup filtered cold water
- 1/2 cup whole or 2% milk
- a few sprinkles of white wine vinegar
- Ground pepper, to taste
- 3 tablespoons minced fresh dill, plus extra dill fronds for garnish
- 3 scallions, white part and some of the green, cut lengthwise most of the way (allow to

remain still attached — this is all to make a finer mince) and sliced finely crosswise
- 1/4 cup shelled unsalted pistachios
- Fresh pomegranate arils, for garnish
- Pita or naan or crisp whole grain crackers as an accompaniment

Direction

- In a small dish, combine the raisins and about 1 cup of warm to hot water. Set aside for 20 minutes or so to plump up, then drain and pat dry with a paper towel.
- While the raisins are soaking, combine the cucumbers and shallots in a small bowl and add the salt. Combine well and allow to sit for 15 minutes. Rinse, drain, and pat dry with a paper towel.
- In a large bowl, combine yogurt, water, and milk; whisk together and season to taste with vinegar, salt, and pepper. You should have a tart taste but not overwhelmingly so. Stir in the dill, scallions, and cucumber mixture. Chill, then ladle into individual bowls, garnishing each with the raisins, pistachios, pomegranate seeds, and dill fronds. Serve as a starter with flatbread as an accompaniment.

31. Corn Chowder With Smoked Salmon And Dill

Serving: Serves 6 | Prep: | Cook: | Ready in:

Ingredients

- 1 small yellow onion, diced
- 1 leek, chopped (white part only)
- 2 cups yukon gold potatoes, peeled and cut into 1/2 inch dice
- 2 tablespoons olive oil
- 2 tablespoons unsalted butter
- 2 ears of corn
- 4 cups organic vegetable stock
- 1 cup heavy cream
- 2 teaspoons kosher salt
- 1 teaspoon black pepper
- 1 teaspoon sweet paprika
- 8 ounces smoked salmon, cut into 1/2 inch pieces
- 1 bunch fresh dill, torn into small sprigs

Direction

- With a sharp knife, scrape the corn kernels from the cobs until you have two cups of kernels.
- Heat the olive oil and butter in a large soup pot over medium heat. Sauté the onion and leek until soft and translucent, about 5 minutes. Stir in the potatoes and cook for 2 minutes, then add the corn and vegetable stock. Bring to a low boil, then turn down the heat and simmer for 15 minutes.
- In two batches, pour half the soup into blender and process until smooth/ Pour the blended soup back into the pot and add cream, salt, pepper and paprika. Bring to a low boil and simmer for 5 minutes Taste for seasoning and adjust as needed. To serve, ladle soup into bowls and top with the smoked salmon and dill.

32. Crab Cake Melt

Serving: Makes 2 open-faced sandwiches | Prep: | Cook: | Ready in:

Ingredients

- 2 teaspoons olive oil
- 2 tablespoons minced shallot
- 1 tablespoon minced red bell pepper
- 1/2 cup jumbo lump crab
- 1/4 teaspoon mustard
- 1/8 teaspoon dried dill
- salt and pepper
- 2-4 tablespoons grated cheese of your choice (I like sharp cheddar or gruyere)
- 2 slices whole-grain bread
- 1/2 small avocado

Direction

- Heat the olive oil in a medium frying pan over medium heat until hot but not smoking. Add the shallots and pepper and fry until golden. Add the crab and season with mustard, dill, salt and pepper. Once hot and slightly browned, remove from heat.
- Toast bread. Spread with a few slices of avocado and mash with a fork. Top with crab mixture, then 1-2 tablespoons shredded cheese. Add to the frying pan over medium heat and cover. Let cook for 2-3 minutes, or until cheese melts (alternatively, broil under high heat, watching carefully, until cheese is melted). Enjoy immediately.

33. Creamy Cucumber Salad With Yogurt And Spice

Serving: Serves 4 | Prep: | Cook: | Ready in:

Ingredients

- 1 large cucumber
- 1 cup whole milk yogurt
- 1 garlic clove, pressed
- 1-2 tablespoons olive oil, plus more for drizzling
- 1 tablespoon chopped mint
- 1 tablespoon chopped dill
- Red pepper flakes

Direction

- Peel the cucumber. Cut it in half lengthwise, then slice into half-moons about 1/3-inch thick. Place in a bowl and season with salt and pepper.
- Add yogurt, garlic, olive oil, mint, and dill, and stir. Refrigerate while you're preparing the rest of your meal–try to give it at least a half an hour.
- Check the seasonings and add more salt and pepper if needed. Transfer to a serving bowl and sprinkle with red pepper flakes and drizzle olive oil over the top.

34. Creamy Dilled Green Bean Salad

Serving: Makes 4 side servings | Prep: | Cook: | Ready in:

Ingredients

- 1 pound green beans (ends trimmed)
- 1 small shallot (minced)
- 1/2 cup mayo
- 1/4 cup Feta cheese (crumbled)
- 1 tablespoon Dijon mustard
- 1 tablespoon apple cider vinegar
- 1 tablespoon fresh dill (minced)
- salt and pepper
- 1 tablespoon olive oil

Direction

- Heat 1 tbsp olive oil in a sauté pan over medium heat. Drop in green beans with a dash of salt. Sauté for 3 minutes. Add 1/4 cup water and cover to steam for 5 minutes. Remove from pan and immerse in ice water to stop the cooking. Drain.
- As green beans cook, stir together shallot, mayo, Feta, Dijon mustard, vinegar, dill, salt and pepper in a mixing bowl. Add green beans and toss to coat.

35. Cucumber Salad

Serving: Serves 4 | Prep: | Cook: | Ready in:

Ingredients

- 1 Large Cucumber
- 1/2 Medium Red Onion
- 1/4 cup Red Wine Vinegar
- 1/4 cup olive oil

- 1 tablespoon Dill
- 1 tablespoon sugar

Direction

- Slice cucumber and red onion.
- In a separate bowl combine sugar and vinegar
- While whisking add olive oil in a stream until the vinaigrette comes together.
- Pour over cucumber and red onion.
- Add dill and salt and pepper to taste.
- Toss

36. Dad's Favourite Baked Fish

Serving: Serves 4 | Prep: | Cook: | Ready in:

Ingredients

- 1 pound frozen tilapia filets
- 1 lemon
- 1 cup mayonnaise [do NOT use reduced fat or no fat varieties]
- 1 1/2 tablespoons onion powder [NOT salt]
- 1/2 teaspoon garlic powder [NOT salt]
- 1 tablespoon dried dill [may substitute 2 tablespoons fresh dill]
- 1 teaspoon coarse ground salt
- 1 teaspoon fresh ground pepper
- 1/3 cup shredded Parmesan cheese
- 16 multigrain saltine crackers, finely crushed

Direction

- Preheat oven to 375 degrees F. Line a rimmed baking sheet with aluminum foil, parchment paper or a silicone baking mat. If using foil or parchment paper, spray lightly with nonstick cooking spray. Place fish filets on prepared baking sheet.
- In a small bowl, zest the lemon. Then, cut the lemon in half and squeeze the juice into the bowl. Add the mayonnaise, onion powder, garlic powder, dill, salt, pepper, and cheese to bowl and whisk thoroughly together.
- Use a spoon to spread mayonnaise mixture evenly over each of the tilapia filets. Sprinkle evenly with saltine crumbs. Place baking pan in oven and bake fish for 15-20 minutes or just until fish baked through and opaque. Switch oven over the broiler and broil for 1-2 minutes or just until top is bubbly and golden brown. Serve immediately.

37. Delicious Cabbage Pie

Serving: Serves 12 | Prep: | Cook: | Ready in:

Ingredients

- Cabbage filling
- 1 medium cabbage head
- 1 medium onion
- 1 teaspoon salt
- 3/4 teaspoons freshly ground black pepper
- 1/2 cup fresh parsley chopped
- 1/4 cup fresh dill chopped
- 1 cup good feta cheese (Greek or French)
- Pie Batter
- 1 cup all purpose flour
- 1 cup sour cream
- 1 cup mayonnaise
- 5 eggs
- 1 teaspoon baking powder
- 1/2 teaspoon baking soda

Direction

- Cabbage filling
- In a large bowl mix shredded cabbage, sliced onion, parsley, dill, salt and pepper, set aside.
- Preheat the oven to 350 degrees. Butter and sprinkle with some breadcrumbs the bottom of a large casserole or glass baking dish.
- Pie Batter
- To a mixing bowl sift the flour, baking powder, baking soda. Mix to combine. In a large measuring cup mix sour cream, mayonnaise and lightly beaten eggs, fold-in to the flour mixture.

- Pour 2/3 of the batter to the baking dish; then squeeze with your hands the excess liquid from cabbage filling and spread it on top of the batter. Crumble feta evenly on the top of the cabbage, then cover with the rest of the batter. Bake for 1 hour, or until the pie is golden brown and the sides are slightly pulled from the baking dish. Serve hot or room temperature.

38. Dill Cucumber Salad With Shaved Machego

Serving: Serves 4 | Prep: | Cook: |Ready in:

Ingredients

- 4 Cucumbers
- 1 cup Fresh Dill Chopped Loosely
- 4 tablespoons Extra Virgin Olive Oil
- 1/2 Squeezed Lemom
- 1 teaspoon Fresh ground sea salt
- 1 teaspoon Fresh ground pepper
- 1/4 pound Manchego, shaven slices

Direction

- Peel the cucumbers and then slice each of them once lengthwise. Then you can line them all up on a large cutting board and cut them horizontally so that you get little halves. I like to keep them slightly thick - just seems to make them better when you crunch into them. But, you can slice them however you prefer.
- Combine the cucumbers and all the other ingredients in a large mixing bowl and toss.
- Refrigerate for, at least, one hour.
- Top with Manchego slices. Serve!
- This is an excellent accompaniment for cold Salmon dishes. I usually serve it with Salmon and a cold couscous salad for an appealing summer luncheon.
- You must use fresh dill for this - dried simply won't work. Chop up the dill loosely, leaving

it in big chunks and it will taste really, really good!

39. Dill Pickle Soup

Serving: Serves 6 | Prep: | Cook: |Ready in:

Ingredients

- 8 cups Chicken stock or broth
- 2 Chicken Bouillon Cubes
- 2 Medium Carrots, coarsely grated
- 2 cups Potatoes, cubed
- 1 cup Celery, thinly sliced
- 5 Large Dill Pickles, grated
- 1/2 cup Milk
- 2 tablespoons Flour
- 1 Egg
- 5 tablespoons Sour Cream, more for serving

Direction

- In a large soup pot, combine the chicken stock, bouillon cubes, carrots, potatoes, and celery. Cook for 10 minutes or just until potatoes are soft. Do not overcook.
- When potatoes are done, add the grated dill pickles and cook another 15 minutes.
- In a small bowl, whisk milk and flour. Add a small amount of hot broth to temper flour and milk, then add to soup pot and stir well. Bring soup to a boil, stirring often until slightly thickened. Remove from heat.
- Beat egg and sour cream together then temper with hot soup. Add tempered mixture to soup and stir till smooth. Do not boil soup but keep warm over low fire. Serve with a dollop of sour cream.

40. Dill And Fennel Frond Potato Salad

Serving: Makes about 6 side servings | Prep: | Cook: | Ready in:

Ingredients

- 6 large redskin potatoes
- 3/4 cup good quality mayo
- 1/2 cup sour cream
- 2 tablespoons minced fennel fronds
- 2 tablespoons minced fresh dill weed
- 1 teaspoon ground fennel seed
- Juice of 1/2 lemon
- 1/2 teaspoon salt
- 1/2 teaspoon black pepper
- 2 tablespoons milk (any kind)
- 1 cup diced celery (small dice)
- 3 green onions/scallions thinly sliced
- Additional mayo if needed
- Additional salt and pepper for re-seasoning

Direction

- Steam or boil the potatoes in their jackets in water until fork tender. This could take between 15 and 20 minutes, depending on potato size.
- While the potatoes are cooking, make the dressing by combining the mayo, sour cream, fennel fronds, dill, ground fennel seed, lemon juice, salt, pepper and milk. Set aside or refrigerate.
- When the potatoes are done, drain them in a colander and then while still warm but cool enough to handle, peel them and then cut them in small chunks and place in a large mixing bowl.
- Gently stir in the celery and green onion and then start stirring in the dressing a little at a time. Depending on your potatoes you may not need all the dressing. You want a nice creamy consistency. If it's too dry, stir in a little more mayo.
- Refrigerate for at least a few hours and when ready to serve, re-season with salt and pepper if you like.

41. Dill And Pea Pilaf

Serving: Serves 4 | Prep: | Cook: | Ready in:

Ingredients

- INGREDIENTS- Rice/chawal - 1.5 cups Dill /suwa -2 bunch,130 gms Tomato -275 gms Peas/matar -1/2 cup Chili powder /lal mirch- 1 tsp Coriander powder /dhaniya 1 tsp Salt /namak - to taste Water- 3 cups Tempering- Cooking oil- 5 tbsp Cumin seeds- 1tsp Cloves

Direction

- Wash and soak rice for 20 minutes.
- Discard the hard steams and wash the dill leaves.
- Now finely chop the dill leaves and tomatoes.
- Heat oil in a heavy and broad pan.
- Add all the tempering and let it crackle.
- Now add chopped tomatoes and salt, cover and cook till tomatoes become soft.
- Add dill leaves and all the spices and sauté.
- When oil start separating then add soaked rice and peas and stir for a minute.
- Now add water in the rice and let it come to a boil.
- When it start boiling cover the pan and let it cook on slow flame till done.
- When done fluff with a fork and serve hot.
- Serving suggestions-best served with yogurt, tomato raita and beetroot raita

42. Dill(icious), Pickled Cucumber And Potato Summer Salad

Serving: Serves a crowd | Prep: | Cook: | Ready in:

Ingredients

- Pickling Marinade
- 4 tablespoons Distilled Vinegar
- 4 tablespoons Apple Cider Vinegar
- 1/2 cup Fresh Dill, plus 2 Tablespoons chopped Fresh Dill
- 1 1/2 tablespoons Kosher Salt
- 2-3 Hothouse Cucumbers, thinly sliced
- Potato and Finishing Steps - Day 2
- 2 1/2 - 3 pounds Yukon Gold potatoes
- 1/2 cup shallots, minced
- 1/2 cup white onion, sliced, then sliced in half again for medium shards
- 4 Red radishes, shredded (optional)
- 4 carrots, shredded (optional)
- 1/2 cup Greek Yogurt
- 2 tablespoons Mayonaise
- Kosher Salt & Fresh Cracked Pepper, to taste

Direction

- Pickling Marinade
- Day One: Stir vinegars and 1 1/2 tablespoons of kosher salt in small bowl until salt dissolves.
- Place sliced cucumbers, 1/2 cup fresh dill in a heavy 1-gallon resealable plastic bag.
- Add vinegar mixture; seal bag. Turn several times to coat. Refrigerate overnight, turning bag occasionally.
- Potato and Finishing Steps - Day 2
- Cook potatoes in large pot of boiling salted water until tender, about 30 minutes. Drain.
- Peel potatoes; quarter lengthwise. Cut crosswise into 1/2-inch-thick slices. Place potatoes in large bowl; sprinkle generously with kosher salt and pepper.
- Place warm, sliced potatoes in colander/sieve under a large bowl. Pour cucumber mixture (shallot, onion, and 3 Tbsp. of dill) over the potatoes and mix well. Take the large bowl under the colander with the brine and repeat; pouring over the potatoes and cucumbers allowing brine to drain away.
- Let stand 1 hour, refrigerated in the colander with a plate underneath. Season to taste with salt and pepper. Empty drained cucumber and potato mixture in a large bowl. Gently mix in yogurt and mayonnaise. At this stage your salad is ready and can be kept in the fridge for the flavors to meld or served immediately.
- To service, place refrigerated potato and cucumber mixture into large bowl. Garnish the salad with shredded carrots and radishes. (Optional)
- Garnish with Fresh Sprigs of Dill (optional)

43. Dilled Zucchini Soup For All Seasons

Serving: Makes about 2 quarts | Prep: | Cook: |Ready in:

Ingredients

- 2 tablespoons butter
- 2 tablespoons extra virgin olive oil
- 1 medium onion, diced
- 4 medium red skin potatoes, peeled and cubed (about 4 cups) or more:see note below
- 1 medium zucchini grated on the large holes of a box grater (about 3 cups)
- 1 teaspoon salt
- 1/2 teaspoon black pepper
- 3 tablespoons minced fresh dill (or 1 tablespoon dried)
- 6 cups chicken broth
- 1/2 cup sour cream
- Thinly sliced green onion for garnish (optional) if serving warm
- Finely diced cucumber for garnish (optional) if serving chilled

Direction

- In a 4 quart soup pot, melt the butter along with the olive oil, add the diced onion and saute until the onion softens but doesn't brown.
- Add the diced potatoes, shredded zucchini, salt, pepper and dill and continue to saute while stirring for 3 or 4 minutes.

- Add the chicken broth, bring up to a boil and then simmer for about 20 minutes until the potatoes are fork tender.
- Cool the soup a bit and then puree with an immersion blender or blend in batches in a regular blender. To serve warm, bring the soup just barely to a boil and whisk in the sour cream Garnish each bowl with the green onion if desired. To serve cold, after whisking in the sour cream, cool the soup to room temperature and then chill in the fridge for several hours (or overnight) before serving and garnish with the cucumber.
- Note: For a thicker soup add a few more potatoes to the mix.

44. Eggplant Pide (or Eggplant Boats)

Serving: Makes 6 eggplant pides | Prep: 0hours10mins | Cook: 0hours35mins | Ready in:

Ingredients

- 3 Eggplants
- 1/2 cup Brown Basmati Rice
- 1.5 cups Red Kidney Beans, cooked (1 can)
- 1/2 cup Fresh Dill, chopped
- 1/4 cup Tomatoes, chopped
- 1/2 teaspoon Sea Salt
- 1/4 teaspoon Pepper
- 1/4 teaspoon Cinnamon
- 2 teaspoons Paprika
- 2 Garlic Cloves
- 1/2 Red Onion, chopped
- 1/4 cup Water
- 2 tablespoons Olive Oil

Direction

- Start by making the brown rice. Add 1 cup of water to ½ cup of rice and bring to boil. Cover and simmer for about 30 minutes or until all water is absorbed.
- Heat up oven to 400F.
- Cut each eggplant lengthwise and scoop out the middle. Save this "middle" part of the eggplant – we will cook it later.
- Spray a little olive oil over the eggplants and sprinkle with salt and pepper. Bake in the oven for 25 mins.
- While eggplants are baking, sauté garlic and onions over medium heat.
- Chop the eggplants that we saved earlier and add it to the pan.
- Add all the spices and stir.
- Once eggplants start to get soft, add tomatoes and water. Stir, cover with lid, reduce heat to medium low and cook for 10 minutes.
- Add cooked brown basmati rice to the mixture along with red kidney beans and dill and stir. Take off the heat
- Take the baked eggplant boats from the oven and start filling them in with the rice and veggie mixture
- You can serve them just like that or pair with vegan tzatziki sauce or simple fit tahini dressing.

45. End Of Season Tomato Salad

Serving: Serves 4 | Prep: | Cook: | Ready in:

Ingredients

- 2-3 ripe tomatoes, cored and sliced 1/4 inch thick
- 1/4 of a medium onion, sliced paper thin (I used a mandoline)
- 1/2 of a medium fennel bulb, sliced paper thin
- 1 tablespoon minced dill
- 2 tablespoons crumbled goat cheese
- 1/2 teaspoon dijon mustard
- 1 teaspoon sherry vinegar
- 3 teaspoons olive oil

Direction

- Arrange the tomato slices on a platter. Top with paper thin onion, fennel, and chopped dill. Season generously with kosher salt. Let sit for at least 30 minutes.
- Crumble goat cheese over top. Mix together the Dijon, sherry vinegar, and olive oil and drizzle over top. Season with freshly ground black pepper.

46. Fish Cakes

Serving: Serves 4 | Prep: | Cook: |Ready in:

Ingredients

- 240 grams salmon fillets
- 2400 grams cubed sweet potato
- 1 piece zest of 1 lemon
- 1 teaspoon mustard
- 1 piece egg
- 1 teaspoon coconut oil
- 1 tablespoon dill, chopped
- 1 tablespoon parsley, chopped
- 4 tablespoons buckwheat flour
- 6 tablespoons ground almonds

Direction

- Peel and chop the sweet potato into small chunks, then place in a pan of water. Bring to the boil then simmer for 20 mins (until softened).
- Meanwhile grill the salmon for 10 minutes (until just cooked).
- Once the potatoes are ready, drain out the water then mash. Mix in the lemon zest, dill, parsley and mustard.
- Break the salmon fillets into flakes, then mix with the potato mixture.
- Divide the mixture into 6 cakes.
- Place the flour, egg and ground almonds in separate bowls.
- Coat each cake in flour, then the egg then the ground almonds.
- Heat the coconut oil in a frying pan, then gently fry the cakes for 3-4 minutes on each side, then serve.

47. Fraiche Start Carrot Quiche

Serving: Makes 1 delicious quiche | Prep: | Cook: |Ready in:

Ingredients

- 1 1/4 cups 3 tablespoons AP flour
- 10 tablespoons unsalted butter (1 stick + 2 tblsp)
- 1/4 teaspoon garlic granules
- 1/4 teaspoon onion powder
- 4-6 tablespoons ice water
- 1 teaspoon safflower or vegetable oil
- 2 medium shallots, thinly sliced
- 2 cups shredded carrots (heirloom preferable)
- 5 eggs
- 1 cup creme fraiche
- 1 cup half and half
- 1/2 teaspoon black pepper
- 1/2 teaspoon dried dill
- 1/2 teaspoon dried mustard
- 2 tablespoons chopped fresh dill

Direction

- To prep for the quiche crust, cut the butter into cubes and put it in the freezer to chill for at least 20 minutes.
- Put 1 1/4 cup of flour, chilled butter, onion powder, garlic, and sugar into a food processor and pulse until combined - flour will begin to look grainier and crumby. Then, add 1 tablespoon of ice water at a time, pulsing until the dough begins to form a ball. Remove the dough and wrap in wax paper and put it into the refrigerator for 1 hour. You can use saran wrap here, but wax paper will help in a following step.
- While dough is chilling, prepare the other ingredients of the tart. Heat the teaspoon of

olive oil in a small pan over medium heat. Sauté shallots until they have softened and let off a sweet aroma, 5 minutes. They are ready when you can't keep your hands off of them. Take off heat and set aside.

- Use a hand grater or food processor to grate your carrots. The finer the grate, the better, but any size will do.
- Place the carrots and shallots into a paper towel, clean dish towel, or cheesecloth and over a sink or bowl, squeeze all the extra water out (as if you are straining homemade cheese). Give it a few big squeezes and then take the carrots and shallots out, and set aside.
- By now, it should be time to remove the dough. Let your dough sit out at room temperature for 5 minutes and preheat your oven to 350 dg F.
- Right on top wax paper that you used, roll out the dough into a 12-inch circle that is 1/8 inch thick. To transfer the dough, simply put your well-greased, 9-inch pie dish upside down over the center of the dough, leaving about 1-2 inch overhang on every side. Gently, with one hand on the pie plate and one under the wax paper, turn the whole thing right side up and then use your hands to press the dough into place. Take off wax paper and fold the overhanging dough under itself, using the tips of your fingers to press the edges into the pie plate, making those decorative indents that I personally always admire.
- Use a fork to make a few prong marks on the bottom of the dough. Put the wax paper back onto the dough and fill the bottom with dried beans or peas or whatever you have to act as an oven-safe weight. Place into oven and bake for 15 minutes. Take out and remove the wax paper/weight combo and bake for another 15 minutes, until the crust begins to turn a golden hue. Take out and cool.
- While the crust rests, prepare your filling. Place 1 egg and the remaining 3 tablespoons of flour in a mixing bowl and mix at high speed. Add the other 4 eggs until well combined.
- In another bowl, whisk together the crème fraiche with half-and-half until smooth. Slowly pour in the egg mixture, whisking in 1/3 at a time. When well combined, add the black pepper, dried dill, dried mustard, and fresh dill. Stir until blended.
- Put the shallot, carrot mixture onto the bottom of your crust and pour in the egg, crème fraiche mixture until it reaches just [1/4] inch below the edge of the crust. Place into oven and bake for 35 minutes or until the quiche has set. Serve with a mimosa. Enjoy.

48. French Lentil And Arugula Salad With Herbed Cashew Cheese

Serving: Serves 4 | Prep: 0hours0mins | Cook: 0hours0mins | Ready in:

Ingredients

- For the salad:
- 1/3 cup olive oil
- 1 small shallot, minced
- 1 teaspoon salt
- 2 tablespoons freshly squeezed lemon juice
- 1 tablespoon Champagne vinegar
- 1 teaspoon Dijon mustard
- 2 1/2 cups cooked Le Puy green lentils, drained well
- 2 cups firmly packed baby arugula leaves
- 1 cup thinly sliced radishes
- 1 cup chopped endive
- 1 cup sliced cucumber
- 1/4 cup chopped fresh dill
- 1/3 cup toasted walnuts, chopped
- 1 dash black pepper
- 1/4 cup herbed cashew cheese (below)
- For the herbed cashew cheese:
- 1 1/2 cups cashew pieces or a combination of cashews and pine nuts, soaked for at least 3 hours and drained
- 2 tablespoons large flake nutritional yeast
- 1 teaspoon salt
- 2 teaspoons herbes de Provence

- 1/4 teaspoon black pepper
- 3 tablespoons freshly squeezed lemon juice
- 1 clove garlic, minced
- 4 tablespoons water, divided

Direction

- For the salad:
- In a small bowl or measuring cup, whisk together the olive oil, shallot, salt, lemon juice, vinegar, and mustard until evenly blended.
- In a large bowl, stir together the lentils, arugula, radishes, endive, cucumber, and dill. Drizzle evenly with the dressing, then toss or stir until all the ingredients are evenly coated. Stir in the walnuts and season with black pepper to taste. Dot the top of the salad with small bits of the cashew cheese (about 1/2 teaspoon each).
- Serve salad right away, or store in an airtight container in the fridge for up to 3 days.
- For the herbed cashew cheese:
- Put the cashews in a food processor or blender (preferably a high-speed blender). Add the nutritional yeast, salt, herbes de Provence, pepper, lemon juice, and garlic. Pulse a few times to break the cashews down until they have a wet, coarse, mealy texture.
- With the motor running, drizzle in 2 tablespoons of the water. Now it's time for some kitchen intuition: Keep adding water, stopping occasionally to scrape down the sides of the work bowl, until the mixture has a good consistency. It should be similar to a thick hummus—a little coarse, but smooth and spreadable. You may not need all of the remaining 2 tablespoons of water. (If using a blender, start on a low speed and gradually increase to high speed as you add the water, using a plunger attachment the entire time to keep the mixture blending.)
- Taste and adjust the seasonings as desired. Stored in a covered container in the fridge, the cheese will keep for about 5 days

49. Fresh Dill Vegetable Dip

Serving: Serves 6 or so | Prep: | Cook: | Ready in:

Ingredients

- 3 tablespoons Fresh Chopped Dill
- 1/2 tablespoon Fresh Chopped Oregano
- 1 teaspoon Salt
- 1/2 teaspoon Pepper
- 1/2 cup Mayonaisse
- 1 cup Sour cream

Direction

- Mix it all together.
- Add more dill, oregano, salt, and pepper to taste. I like to go heavy on the dill, almost doubling the amount.

50. Fresh Tomato Sandwich

Serving: Serves 1 | Prep: 0hours0mins | Cook: 0hours0mins | Ready in:

Ingredients

- 2 slices good bread
- 1 ripe tomato
- 1 onion
- 1 tablespoon Mayo
- 3 Springs of Fresh Dill
- Salt & pepper

Direction

- Toast & butter the bread. Spread one slice with Mayo
- Slice the tomato & onion and place a layer of each on one side of the toast
- Sprinkle the tomato with salt & pepper & top with the Dill
- Cut the sandwich in 2 or 3 pieces and enjoy!

51. Gatsby's Harlequin Salad

Serving: Serves 6-8 | Prep: | Cook: | Ready in:

Ingredients

- Buttermilk Corn Salad
- 6 ears of sweet corn, husks and silks removed
- 1/2 small, overly ripe red pepper, small dice
- 1 cup greek yogurt
- 1 cup buttermilk
- coarse salt and fresh pepper, to taste
- 1 tablespoon fresh dill, finely minced
- 8-10 asparagus spears
- Caprese salad
- 8 ounces grape tomatoes
- 4 ounces mini mozzarella pearls
- 2 tablespoons basil, snipped
- 2 tablespoons olive oil
- 1 tablespoon balsamic vinegar
- coarse salt and fresh pepper, to taste

Direction

- In a large, wide pan, simmer your asparagus for 2-3 minutes. I had nice thick stalks...remove and plunge into a large, wide bowl filled with ice and water to "shock". When cool to the touch, place on paper towels to drain. Chill until ready to assemble
- Cut corn off the cob and "milk" the cob by running the back edge of the knife over the cob to release the corn milk.
- Add diced red pepper, dill, yogurt and buttermilk. Stir and season with salt and pepper to taste. Chill until ready to assemble.
- Prepare caprese salad by chopping tomatoes and cheese, tossing in oil, vinegar and basil. Season with salt and pepper. Chill.
- To assemble, on a long rectangular serving dish, arrange spears in a crisscross pattern to create a harlequin design...with diamond shapes in the middle and triangles framing the sides.
- Fill in diamonds with corn mixture and triangles with caprese mix.
- If you have any leftovers...or just not in the mood for the fussiness of the 'harlequin'...drain excess liquid from the corn and tomato salads, cut the asparagus spears into bite sized pieces and mix together the salads and spears.

52. Gena Hamshaw's (Vegan) Deli Bowls With Smashed Chickpea Salad

Serving: Serves 4 | Prep: 0hours20mins | Cook: 0hours0mins | Ready in:

Ingredients

- Deli Bowls with Smashed Chickpea Salad
- 3 cups cooked chickpeas, or 2 (15-ounce, or 425g) cans, drained and rinsed
- 2 stalks celery, finely chopped
- 2 scallions, green parts only, chopped
- 1 large dill pickle, finely chopped
- 2 tablespoons chopped fresh dill, or 2 teaspoons dried dill weed
- 1 tablespoon capers (optional)
- 6 tablespoons (90g) tahini or vegan mayonnaise, plus more if needed
- 1 tablespoon apple cider vinegar
- 1 1/2 tablespoons Dijon mustard
- 1/4 teaspoon salt
- Freshly ground black pepper
- 5 cups (150g) firmly packed baby spinach, baby arugula, or chopped lettuce
- 2 cups (300g) cherry tomatoes, halved or quartered
- 1 large cucumber, peeled and chopped
- 3/4 cup (175ml) Everyday Lemon Tahini Dressing (see below)
- 4 whole wheat pita breads, cut into quarters, or 4 slices rye, pumpernickel, or sourdough toast, cut into quarters
- Optional toppings: Chopped dill pickles, sauerkraut, pickled beets, chopped scallions
- Everyday Lemon Tahini Dressing

- 1/4 cup (60ml) warm water, plus more if desired
- 1/4 cup (60g) tahini
- 1 clove garlic, finely minced or grated
- 2 tablespoons freshly squeezed lemon juice
- 1/2 teaspoon agave nectar or maple syrup
- 1/4 teaspoon salt
- 1/8 teaspoon freshly ground black pepper

Direction

- Deli Bowls with Smashed Chickpea Salad
- To make the chickpea salad, put the chickpeas into a large bowl and use a potato masher or a fork to mash them partially, leaving about half of the chickpeas whole. Add the celery, scallions, pickle, dill, capers, tahini, vinegar, mustard, and salt and mix well. Add a little bit more tahini if needed to hold the mixture together. Season with pepper, then taste and adjust the seasonings. Toast the pita, if desired.
- To serve, divide the lettuce, tomatoes, and cucumber among four bowls. Drizzle with the dressing and top with the pita wedges and one-quarter of the chickpea salad. Serve right away, offering any other desired toppings at the table.
- Everyday Lemon Tahini Dressing
- To make the dressing, combine all the ingredients in a small bowl or measuring cup and whisk until evenly blended. If the dressing is thicker than you'd like, whisk in water by the tablespoonful to achieve the desired consistency. (Stored in an airtight container in the refrigerator, the dressing will keep for 1 week.)

53. Goats Cheese & Aubergine Quinoa Oat Crust Pizza

Serving: Serves 2 | Prep: | Cook: | Ready in:

Ingredients

- Quinoa-Oat Crust Ingredients
- 1/2 teaspoon freshly ground black pepper
- 1/2 teaspoon maldon salt
- 1 tablespoon chia seeds
- 1/3 cup water
- 2 tablespoons flax seeds
- 6 rosemary leaves (chopped)
- 1 cup quinoa flakes
- 1/4 cup milled oats
- 1/3 cup olive oil
- 1 organic egg
- 1/4 cup gluten free brown flour
- 1 teaspoon organic honey
- 3 pitted olives
- Toppings
- 60 grams soft herbed goats cheese
- 1 small eggplant cut into long slices
- 2 tablespoons virgin olive oil
- 3 tablespoons freshly chopped parsley
- 1/2 teaspoon freshly ground black pepper
- 1/4 teaspoon maldon sea salt
- 1/4 cup goat yogurt
- 1 roasted garlic
- 1/2 teaspoon sumac
- 1/2 teaspoon dill
- 1/2 teaspoon thyme
- 1/2 teaspoon oregano
- 1/2 teaspoon chili

Direction

- Directions for the crust: Preheat the oven to 180 C / 355 F
- In a bowl combine the chia with the water and let that sit for about 2 minutes [while this is happening, chop the rosemary and olives]
- Add in the rest of the ingredients and mix until you have a dough that can be rolled into a ball and doesn't fall apart instantly- if it does add a bit more quinoa flakes/brown flour [but 1 tablespoon at a time- you don't want to overdo it]
- Lightly oil a tart pan, or pie dish- basically anything with a bottom that pops up and place the pan on top of a baking sheet- in case any oil leaks out

- Put the dough in the pan and spread with your hands until the pan is evenly covered [there should be a little more than enough left over depending on pan size]
- Cook the crust for 10-15 minutes- depending on how soft/crunchy you like your crust- keep an eye on it
- While the crust is baking, lightly oil and cook the eggplant on a nonstick pan above medium-high heat until golden brown on each side [salt and pepper to taste]
- Turn off the oven and place the pan on a heat proof surface
- When the crust comes out of the oven place the goat cheese on top and let melt a bit before spreading with the underside of a spoon
- Place the eggplant on the pizza evenly
- Mix the goat yogurt, roasted garlic pieces, sumac, dill, thyme, oregano, chili together and add dollops of the mixture over the eggplant and then sprinkle parsley over the pizza

54. Greek Lemon Soup — Avgolemono

Serving: Serves 4 to 6 | Prep: 0hours0mins | Cook: 0hours0mins | Ready in:

Ingredients

- Soup
- 8 cups homemade or store-bought chicken stock, divided
- 1 1/2 teaspoons kosher salt
- 1/2 teaspoon white pepper
- 1 1/2 cups orzo
- 1 dash sugar
- Lemon Egg Mixture & Garnish
- 4 eggs (whites and yolks separated), room temperature, such as Eggland's Best
- 3 large lemons, juiced
- 1/4 cup finely chopped fresh dill
- 1 dill sprig per serving (fresh thyme, mint, or chives may be used)
- 4 to 6 paper-thin lemon slices (1 per serving)

Direction

- To prepare the soup, bring stock to a boil in a large saucepan. Lower heat to a simmer and add salt, pepper, and orzo; cook until al dente, about 8 minutes. Remove from heat. Set aside 2 cups of stock.
- To prepare the lemon-egg mixture, beat egg whites in a medium-size bowl until soft peaks form. (You can do this with a handheld mixer [on medium] or with a stand mixer.) Beat in the egg yolks and lemon juice. Pour 2 cups of reserved hot stock slowly into the lemon and egg mixture, whisking continuously until all is incorporated. Return soup to medium-low heat and whisk in lemon-egg mixture. Add chicken stock back into the soup and simmer until thickened slightly, about 20 minutes.
- To serve the soup, ladle into warm bowls and garnish with white pepper, chopped dill, a dill sprig, and sliced lemon.

55. Greek Yogurt Potato Salad

Serving: Serves 6 | Prep: 0hours25mins | Cook: 0hours20mins | Ready in:

Ingredients

- 2 pounds red potatoes (5 to 6 ounces each)
- 6 tablespoons kosher salt, plus more to taste
- 1 cup full-fat Greek yogurt
- 2 tablespoons extra-virgin olive oil
- 1/2 cup chopped dill, plus its finely chopped stems
- 1/2 cup chopped mint
- 1/2 cup pitted, torn (or roughly chopped) oil-cured olives

Direction

- Bring a large pot of water (figure about 6 quarts) to a boil. When it starts to simmer, season it with 6 tablespoons kosher salt (I estimate 1 tablespoon kosher salt per quart water).

- While that's heating up, cut the potatoes into eighths—or whatever fraction will give you roughly equally sized potato pieces. Add the potato pieces to the boiling water, then adjust the heat to a simmer. (Simmering, not boiling, the potatoes means they're less likely to fall apart.) Cook until the potatoes are just knife-tender (they'll continue to cook a bit out of the water), starting to check frequently after 10 minutes. When they're done, drain the potatoes into a colander, rinse with cold water to cool, then let them drain until dry.
- While the potatoes are cooking, combine the yogurt and olive oil in a large bowl. Stir to combine. Add the herbs and olives on top (no need to stir yet).
- When the potatoes are cool, add them to the bowl with the yogurt. Stir as gently as possible, taking care to not mash the potatoes. Taste and adjust the seasoning as needed.
- You can serve right away or stick it in the fridge for later.

56. Grilled Calf's Or Beef Liver Served With A Famous Romanian Sauce Mujdei

Serving: Serves 4-6 | Prep: | Cook: | Ready in:

Ingredients

- For the Mujdei sauce (Makes 1 cup)
- • 1 bunch parsley, leaves finely chopped
- • 1 bunch dill, fronds finely chopped
- • 2-3 large garlic cloves, finely minced or pressed
- • 1/4 cup sherry vinegar
- • About 1 1/2 teaspoons coarse salt
- • 1/2 teaspoon red pepper flakes
- • 1/2 teaspoon freshly ground black pepper
- • 1/2 cup strong concentrated chicken broth, at room temperature
- For the marinade; marinating and grilling liver
- • Juice of 2 lemons
- • 3 tablespoons olive oil
- • 1/2 cup dry sherry wine
- • 1 teaspoon fresh ginger, finely ground
- • 1/4 teaspoon red pepper flakes
- • 2 tablespoons fresh parsley, chopped
- • 2 pounds calf's or beef liver, cut into about 1 to1 1/2-inch thick slices
- • 1/2 cup melted butter
- • Salt and freshly ground pepper to taste

Direction

- For the Mujdei sauce (Makes 1 cup)
- Place the parsley, dill and garlic in a medium mixing bowl and toss to combine. Add the vinegar, salt, red and black pepper and stir. Pour in the chicken broth and mix until well combined. Let sit for 30 minutes so that the flavors blend.
- For the marinade; marinating and grilling liver
- To make the marinade: Juice the lemons and place the juice into a glass bowl; add the olive oil, sherry wine, parsley, ginger and red pepper flakes to the bowl and mix the ingredients well.
- Rinse the liver with hot water and loosen the membrane covering the meat with your fingers. As you hold the liver under hot running water, pull the membrane off the liver and discard it. Place the liver into a shallow dish.
- Pour the marinade over the liver, and flip it several times to coat all sides with the marinade. Cover the dish with plastic wrap and place it in the refrigerator. Chill the liver in the refrigerator for about two hours.
- Preheat a charcoal or gas grill to medium-high. Remove the liver from the glass dish; discard the marinade and dry very well with pepper towels.
- Dip liver slices in the melted butter. Place on the grill about 4 inches above the fire. Grill until liver is browned, for about 3 minutes per side. Turn once. Do not overcook; it should be still pink inside.

- Remove from grill to a serving platter, sprinkle with salt and pepper and tent with foil for about 10-15 minutes; then, if you like, slice into thinner slices on a bias. Serve with the mujdei sauce. Grilled or sautéed in oil and butter onions and mushrooms is a very traditional side dish for liver.

57. Grilled Portabello Gyros

Serving: Serves 4 | Prep: | Cook: |Ready in:

Ingredients

- Mushrooms
- 2 to 4 depending on size portobello mushrooms, cleaned, stems removed, and cut in half
- 1/2 cup balsamic vinegar
- 2 cloves garlic, minced.
- 2 sprigs fresh thyme
- 1 teaspoon each salt and freshly ground black pepper
- 2 tablespoons olive oil
- 1/2 teaspoon dried oregano
- Accoutrements
- 1 cup labneh, or full-fat Greek yogurt
- 2 cloves garlic, pulverized
- Zest of one lemon
- 1 tablespoon fresh dill
- 1 teaspoon fresh mint, chiffonade
- 1 tablespoon olive oil
- 1/2   seedless cucumber, shredded
- 1/2 teaspoon salt
- 1   shallot, sliced thinly
- 1 red pepper (you can grill this as well) or tomato
- 4 pita bread wraps

Direction

- Combine all mushroom ingredients, and marinate up to overnight, but at least 30 minutes. Preheat grill.
- Combine labneh or yogurt with garlic, mint, dill, and olive oil. Sprinkle salt over cucumber shreds, let sit 10 minutes then squeeze out the water and add to yogurt. Add lemon zest and stir. This can be made a day before. Refrigerate.
- Grill mushrooms over a medium-high area of your grill, adjusting coals as necessary — or, if using gas, set to medium-high. Cook mushrooms about 5 minutes on each side, then set aside.
- Warm pitas over grill till lightly toasty and malleable. Slice mushrooms thinly, then divide them between the pitas. Add tomatoes or red peppers, sliced shallots, and yogurt mixture (tzatiki), fold, and enjoy!

58. Grilled Stuffed Portabello Mushroom Burgers

Serving: Serves 2 | Prep: | Cook: |Ready in:

Ingredients

- 3   portobello mushrooms
- 1/2   bell pepper
- 1   shallot
- 2 garlic cloves
- 1 teaspoon grapeseed oil
- 2 tablespoons fresh dill, chopped
- 2 ounces smoked cheddar, shredded
- Kosher Salt
- Cayenne Pepper
- 1/4 cup mayo
- 2   brioche buns
- sliced tomatoes
- baby spinach

Direction

- Wipe mushrooms clean with a damp paper towel. Remove stems and scoop gills out. Set the two prettiest mushroom caps aside. Take the 3rd (ugly) mushroom cap, slice it into large

- pieces and chop finely in a food processor. Place chopped mushrooms aside in a bowl.
- Cut the bell pepper and shallot into large pieces, and place along with one garlic clove into the food processor and finely chop.
- Heat grape seed oil in a sauté pan and sauté bell pepper mixture until soft - about 5 minutes. Add chopped mushroom and continue to sauté until most of the liquid is evaporated.
- Place sautéed vegetables back in bowl and stir in the shredded smoked cheddar and one tbsp. of the chopped dill. Season to taste with salt and cayenne pepper.
- Heat a grill to medium heat (about 400) and grill the whole mushroom caps stem side down. This is very important – if you start with stem side up, the cap will collect juices and you'll have to drain it before you can continue. Grill for 7 minutes, then transfer them to a plate and fill with sautéed cheese mixture. Place back on grill, filling side up, for another 5 minutes.
- While the mushrooms are grilling, toast your brioche buns under the broiler for a minute or two until they are golden brown. Also it's now time to make the yummy sauce that goes on the burgers - mix the mayo, remaining chopped dill and the last garlic clove (pressed or minced) in a small bowl. Season with pepper to taste and refrigerate until you are ready to serve.
- When the mushrooms are done grilling, spread the toasted brioche buns with the garlic dill sauce, place the stuffed mushrooms on the buns, and top with fresh tomatoes and spinach.
- Enjoy!

59. Habanero Dill Pickles

Serving: Makes 8 16 oz. mason jars | Prep: | Cook: | Ready in:

Ingredients

- for the brine:
- 8 mason jars
- 6 cups water
- 3 cups apple cider vinegar
- 1/2 cup pickling or sea salt
- 1/4 cup granulated sugar
- per jar:
- 2-3 pickling cucumbers (1/4 inch chips)
- 2 small sprigs fresh dill
- 1 clove garlic (crushed)
- 1 teaspoon dill seed
- 1 tablespoon mustard seeds
- 1 teaspoon caraway seeds
- 1 tablespoon black peppercorns
- 1 teaspoon white peppercorns
- 1 habanero (stem removed)

Direction

- In a medium pot, bring water, vinegar, salt and sugar to a boil. Remove from heat and let cool to room temperature.
- As the brine cools, get the jars ready. Stuff each jar with fresh dill, dill seed, garlic, mustard seeds, caraway seeds, peppercorns, habanero and cucumber chips. Note: I don't sterilize my jars because I keep them in the fridge.
- When liquid has cooled, pour enough in each jar to fill 1/4 inch from the top. Seal with lid and refrigerate. You can eat them as soon as the next day, or wait a couple of weeks before cracking it open. I think you guys are gonna like this one.

60. Herring Salad

Serving: Serves 8-12 | Prep: | Cook: | Ready in:

Ingredients

- 12 ounce jar pickled herring and onions, or freshly pickled, cut into 1/2 inch dice

- 6 tablespoons chopped (1/4 inch dice) dill or half-sour pickles
- 3 medium size waxy potatoes steamed, peeled, cooled and cut into 1/2 inch dice
- 1 crisp tart apple, peeled and cut into 1/2 inch dice
- 1/4 cup finely chopped red onion
- 1/3 cup finely chopped walnuts
- 2 tablespoons white wine vinegar or cider vinegar
- 1/4 cup sour cream
- 1 tablespoon finely chopped fresh dill
- 1 teaspoon Dijon mustard or ¼ teaspoon mustard powder
- 1/2 teaspoon kosher salt, or to taste
- 1/8 teaspoon ground black pepper, or to taste
- 1 tablespoon neutral-flavored oil

Direction

- Combine the herring, pickles, potatoes, apple, onion and walnuts in a 2 or 3 quart serving bowl.
- Combine the vinegar, sour cream, dill, mustard, salt and pepper in a small bowl and whisk to blend. Whisk in the oil. Pour the dressing over the salad, and gently mix. Refrigerate until you are ready to serve it.

61. Homemade Labneh

Serving: Makes 2 1/2 cups | Prep: | Cook: | Ready in:

Ingredients

- Labneh
- 6 cups plain Greek yogurt
- 1 teaspoon sea salt
- 1 tablespoon aji pepper paste
- Toppings
- 10-15 roasted hazelnut chopped into small pieces
- few sprigs of dill, chopped
- 2 tablespoons pomegranate seeds
- 1 tablespoon sumac
- extra virgin olive oil

Direction

- Labneh
- Use a large square of cheesecloth.
- Place over strainer or colander
- In another bowl mix yogurt, salt and pepper paste.
- Put mixture into a strainer with cheesecloth and tide. Put everything over a large bowl in refrigerator for 1-2 days. The longer that the cheese is left, the firmer it becomes.
- Toppings
- Fill a serving dish with labneh.
- Sprinkle hazelnut, dill, pomegranate seeds and sumac over the labneh.
- Drizzle some good olive oil over everything.
- Serve with pita chips, vegetables and fruit.

62. Horseradish Hummus

Serving: Serves 6 | Prep: | Cook: | Ready in:

Ingredients

- 1 cup dried chickpeas, soaked overnight in water or for at least 3 hours
- 1/3 cup Tahini plus 1 tablespoon
- 2 large garlic cloves minced
- juice of 1 large lemon
- 4 tablespoons water
- 1/3 cup olive oil
- 1 teaspoon salt
- 1 bunch fresh dill
- 2 tablespoons prepared horseradish
- crudites for serving

Direction

- Place soaked chickpeas in a small pot with fresh water. Bring chickpeas to a boil and then reduce heat to a simmer. Simmer for at least one hour. You may need to add more water as you simmer the chickpeas ~ check every so

- often to make sure there is an inch or so of water covering them. Once the chickpeas are fork tender, drain them from the water.
- Add the chickpeas, tahini, garlic, lemon juice, water, olive oil, salt, fresh dill and horseradish to a large food processor. Pulse until the consistency becomes smooth. If needed, add more water or olive oil to achieve desired consistency. Serve with crudités and enjoy!

63. Hungarian Creamed Zucchini (Anyu's Tök Fözelék)

Serving: Serves 4 | Prep: | Cook: | Ready in:

Ingredients

- 2 pounds Cleaned Zucchini or summer squash
- Salt
- 2 Bell peppers, one red, one green
- 1 Hot pepper
- 1 tablespoon Vegetable oil
- 1 Clove garlic, crushed
- Pinch Caraway seed
- 2 teaspoons Sweet paprika
- 1 pint Sour cream
- 2 tablespoons All-purpose flour
- 1/4 cup Chopped dill
- Salt and pepper

Direction

- Any size zucchini will do, but if yours is large, remove the large seeds before proceeding. Shred the zucchini on the largest holes of a box grater; the shredding blade of a food processor also works well. You want to end up with about 2 lbs. of shredded zucchini. In a large sieve set over a bowl, layer the zucchini, salting each layer well. Set aside for at least 30 minutes to drain, tossing occasionally.
- Meanwhile, julienne the bell and hot peppers. In a skillet large enough to hold all ingredients, heat the oil. Add the garlic, peppers, caraway, and a pinch of salt and sauté until just softened. Remove from the pan and set aside.
- Add more oil to the skillet and heat gently. Squeeze the zucchini, a handful at a time, removing as much liquid as possible. I use a potato ricer for this job, but you can simply use your hands or wring out the zucchini in a dish towel. Add the zucchini to the warmed skillet.
- Once you've added all the zucchini, turn up the heat to medium and sauté the zucchini, stirring, until the liquid is evaporated. Do not brown! Add the sautéed pepper mixture and the paprika and stir well.
- At this stage, the zucchini can be stored; pack tightly into freezer safe containers or freezer bags, removing as much air as possible, chill, and then freeze until needed. Heat gently when ready to eat.
- Finish the dish: add the 2 Tbs. of flour directly into the sour cream container and whisk until smooth. Stir the sour cream into the hot (not boiling) zucchini mixture and whisk until smooth. Simmer about 2 minutes until it thickens slightly and the flour no longer tastes raw.
- Stir in the dill, adjust the seasonings, and enjoy.

64. Jane Grigson's Celery Soup

Serving: Serves 4, 6 if the rest of the meal is fairly copious | Prep: 0hours15mins | Cook: 0hours57mins | Ready in:

Ingredients

- 1/2 pound celery, chopped (outside stalks or celeriac -- about 2 cups)
- 1/2 cup chopped onion
- 1/2 cup diced potato
- 6 tablespoons butter
- 4 cups turkey or chicken stock
- 1/2 cup milk (optional, up to 1 cup)

- 1 teaspoon dill weed (2 teaspoons for fresh dill)
- 2 1/2 tablespoons cream

Direction

- Stew celery, onion, and potato gently in the butter in a covered pan for 10 minutes. Don't let the vegetables brown. Add stock or water and 1/2 teaspoon of dill weed. Simmer for 20 minutes if you have a blender, 40 minutes if you use a food mill.
- Blend or purée the soup. Pour through a strainer into a clean pan (to remove the last few threads of celery), adding a little milk if too thick. Bring slowly to just under the boil, seasoning with salt, pepper and more dill weed if required.
- Put the cream into the soup dish, and pour the soup in on top. Swirl round with the ladle before serving, to mix in the cream.

65. Jazzed Up Peas, Lemon And Pearl Onions

Serving: Serves 8-10 | Prep: | Cook: | Ready in:

Ingredients

- 3 tablespoons extra-virgin olive oil, and extra for drizzling on top
- 4 and 1/2 tablespoons unsalted butter
- 1 -20 ounces package frozen pearl onions, defrosted
- 1 teaspoon sugar
- 1/2 lemon, juiced
- 5-6 thin slices of lemon
- 2 -16 ounces packages frozen peas, defrosted
- 1 lemon, zested
- Kosher salt and freshly ground black pepper to taste
- 1/4 cup Italian flat-leaf parsley, roughly chopped
- 2 heaping tablespoons fresh dill, roughly chopped
- 1 cup fresh pea shoots, rinsed and dried thoroughly

Direction

- Heat 3 tablespoons olive oil with the butter in a large sauté pan over medium heat until the butter melts.
- Add the pearl onions, sugar, and lemon juice and cook, stirring frequently, until the onions are browned, 5 to 6 minutes.
- Add the lemon slices, peas, and lemon zest and continue cooking until the peas are hot.
- Place in a serving bowl, drizzle with extra-virgin olive oil, and add the parsley and dill.
- Combine gently and season generously with salt and pepper to taste. Scatter the pea shoots on top, folding in a bit, and serve.

66. Kale Salad With Buttermilk Anchovy Dressing

Serving: Serves 2-4 | Prep: | Cook: | Ready in:

Ingredients

- Dressing
- 3 large clove garlic
- the zest of 1 medium organic lemon (on micro plane)
- 2 medium organic lemons, juiced
- 1/2 cup buttermilk (we used Kalona SuperNatural 2%)
- 5 anchovy filets
- 1/2 cup grated, packed Pecorino Romano (grated on the widest side of a box grater)
- 4 egg yolks (pastured eggs if possible)
- 1/4-1/2 cups extra virgin olive oil
- 1/4 teaspoon pink Himalayan salt
- Salad
- 2 medium bunches of lacinato kale (chiffonade or tear with stems removed, rinsed and drained, preferably with a salad spinner)
- 1/2 bunch green onion (roots removed and outer layer peeled, thinly sliced)

- 1/4 cup fresh dill, cleaned and stemmed, roughly chopped
- 1/4 cup fresh parsley, cleaned and stemmed, roughly chopped
- Smoked wild King salmon - about 1/8th lb. per person
- 4-6   pastured eggs (1 or 2 per person)
- 1 teaspoon baking soda

Direction

- Dressing
- Blend all ingredients on high to combine. Add additional salt or anchovies to taste.
- Salad
- Put cleaned kale in a large bowl and add a decent amount of the dressing (2 or 3 tablespoons). Massage the kale well, until it has begun to soften.
- Add in the dill, parsley, and green onions. Toss to combine.
- Fill a medium saucepan halfway with cold water. Stir in the baking soda and bring to a boil.
- When water is at a rolling boil, reduce to a simmer and gently add eggs one by one.
- Allow to continue to simmer for 5 to 6 minutes, depending on desired doneness/runniness.
- Remove from heat and rinse under cold water for 30-60 seconds.
- Peel eggs under cold running water and set aside.
- Plate the salads and top with rolls of the smoked salmon, chopped herbs and green onions.
- Top with a halved (lengthwise) soft boiled egg and freshly cracked black pepper. Add additional dressing if desired!

67. Kale And Red Lettuce Salad W/ Goat Cheese, Pickled Cherries And Grilled Chicken

Serving: Serves 4 | Prep: | Cook: | Ready in:

Ingredients

- 1 cup Chopped Kale
- 1 bunch Red Lettuce
- 1 ounce Goat Cheese
- 3   Chicken Breasts, Chopped
- 1/2 cup Cherries, Seeded and Halved
- 3 cups White Vinegar
- 1.5 cups Water
- 2 cups Sugar
- 1 cup Salt
- 3 tablespoons Dill Seed
- 3 tablespoons Mustard Seed
- 1 pinch Crushed Red Pepper

Direction

- Bring pickling liquid (vinegar, water, salt, sugar, dill seed, mustard seed, and crushed red pepper) to a boil, and stir to make sure all sugar and salt is dissolved. Allow the liquid to cool, then strain into mason jars and fill with cherries. Allow to sit in the pickling liquid anywhere from 1 hour to 12 hours.
- Bake chicken in a 350 degree oven for about 25-35 minutes, until cooked.
- Combine chopped kale, lettuce, goat cheese, chicken and cherries and dress lightly with vinaigrette of your choosing.

68. Kosher Pickles

Serving: Serves lots | Prep: | Cook: | Ready in:

Ingredients

- Vegetables. Cucumbers work extremely well, but so do carrots and cauliflower. Anything firm will do.

- Salt. Kosher salt works well here.
- Water. Filtered is good, to get rid of the chlorine. Chlorine kills bacteri
- Flavouring agents, such as garlic, herbs or spices. Dill is the choice of the traditionalist here.
- Wine, oak or sour cherry leaves (optional).
- A crock pot, ideally earthenware but food grade plastic will do. If you are using an old pot make sure that the glaze is lead free.

Direction

- That's it. Everything else is really easy.
- Clean and trim the vegetables. Cucumbers keep whole, carrots peel and slice, cauliflower break into flowers.
- Clean the pickling pot with a 5% bleach solution or in the dishwasher. Rinse thoroughly.
- Put wine/oak/cherry leaves into the pot. The tannin in the leaves will help with keeping your pickles crunchy.
- Add dill, garlic, etc. Black pepper work well, so does allspice.
- Add the vegetables and cover with water. Be careful to measure the water, you'll need to know the volume so you can add the correct amount of salt.
- Add enough salt to create a 5% saline solution – 25g of salt for every liter of water – and stir. Cover the pickles with a clean plate and weigh down with a food grade plastic bag filled with water and salt.
- Next, store the pot in a cool place, below 21°Celsius or 71° F. Above that temperature our good bacteria run the risk of being overrun by the baddies of the bacterial world, spoiling the pot. That's part of the reason why pickles traditionally got started in fall, with the cooler temperatures arrives a better environment for the preservation of food – kind of useful when you think that winter will be next. Check the pickles every day. Remove all scum and/or mold that may form at the top. If you've kept your pot clean and your pickles submerged you should have little to worry about, but a little bit of growth is perfectly normal. Remove with a paper towel and make sure to wash your hands – this is an occasion where you need to be scrupulously clean – before touching the pot. After a week or so taste your first pickle. It should be firm and crunchy and taste mildly sour. Over the coming weeks the sour flavor will increase, until the pickles are fully fermented and the flavor will stabilize. When taking pickles out of the brine, always use clean tongs, never your hands. You've got a delicate eco-system in your pot, make sure not to disturb it if you can possibly help it. Vegetables preserves with lacto acidic bacteria have a depth and layerdness of flavor that vinegar pickles can only dream about. As per usual, and this is for Mr. Stephenson, time is the magic ingredient here. Time to allow the flavor to develop, time to allow the vegetables to hanker down for the long, cold winter months.

69. Lamb Dolmas (Stuffed Grape Leaves)

Serving: Makes 24-28 dolmas | Prep: | Cook: | Ready in:

Ingredients

- 7 tablespoons extra virgin olive oil
- 1 Small Onion, minced
- 1 pound Grass fed, organic ground lamb
- 1/2 teaspoon dried dill
- 6 tablespoons dried currants
- 1 teaspoon nutmeg
- 1/2 teaspoon cinnamon
- 1 teaspoon cumin
- 8 ounces jar of grape leaves
- 1-2 tablespoons fresh lime juice
- Water
- several thin slices of lemon
- 2-3 bay leaves
- handful of sliced almonds

Direction

- Heat 3 tablespoons olive oil in a large skillet. Add the onion and sauté until transparent. (You may add a little water to keep from browning onions). Add the ground lamb and cook completely. About half way through cooking the lamb, add the dill, currants, nutmeg, cinnamon, and cumin. Remove the pan from the heat and allow the mixture to cool for a few minutes.
- Place a grape leaf on a plate, vein side up. Place 1-2 heaping teaspoons of the filling in the center of each grape leaf. Cut the stem from the leaf if there is one. Fold the sides of the leaves over the filling and roll gently from the bottom to the top. Arrange the dolmas in a baking dish.
- Mix together the lime juice, remaining olive oil, and water to equal one cup of liquid. Pour over the dolmas. Top with several slices of lemon or lime and 2 or 3 bay leaves. Sprinkle with a few sliced almonds. Layer any remaining grape leaves on top. Cover loosely with foil. Bake at 350 ° for 45 minutes or until the liquid is almost completely absorbed.

70. Lamb Stuffed Peppers

Serving: Serves 4 | Prep: | Cook: | Ready in:

Ingredients

- 1/4 cup brown rice
- 1/4 cup millet
- 1/4 cup red lentils
- 1 1/2 cups water
- 2 bay leaves
- 1/2 teaspoon smoked paprika
- 1/2 cup diced onion
- 2 teaspoons oil (I used grapeseed oil)
- 1 large tomato
- 1/2 cup roughly-chopped fresh dill, plus a little extra for garnish
- 1/2 pound ground lamb
- 1/4 cup crumbled feta
- 1 lemon
- salt
- pepper

Direction

- Preheat your oven to 350 degrees.
- Add rice, millet, lentils, water, bay leaves, paprika, and a pinch of salt to a large sauce pan. Bring to a boil and then reduce heat to low and cover.
- While rice mixture is beginning to cook, heat a skillet over medium-low add the oil and cook the onions until browned. Stir the cooked onions into the rice mixture.
- Add the diced tomato and 1/2 cup of chopped dill to the rice mixture.
- Heat the skillet to medium-high and add the ground lamb and season with salt and pepper. There should still be enough oil in the skillet from cooking the onions, but add a little more if it seems necessary. Cook the meat until browned and add to the rice mixture.
- Continue to cook the rice mixture until it has absorbed almost all of the liquid (i.e. it shouldn't be runny). Remove the bay leaves from the stuffing before stuffing peppers.
- While the rice mixture finishes cooking, cut the peppers in half from stem to base and remove the stem and seeds. Fill each half generously with stuffing mixture and arrange in the skillet. Cover with aluminum foil and bake in the oven for 45 minutes.
- Squeeze a little lemon juice over peppers and top with feta and extra dill to garnish.

71. Latke And Smoked Salmon Stacks

Serving: Serves 6 to 8 | Prep: | Cook: | Ready in:

Ingredients

- 1 cup plain Greek yogurt

- 1/2 hothouse cucumber, grated and squeezed dry
- 1 tablespoon fresh lemon juice
- 1 tablespoon extra-virgin olive oil
- 1 tablespoon chopped dill
- Kosher salt
- Freshly ground black pepper
- 3 pounds russet potatoes, peeled and grated
- 1/4 cup vegetable oil
- 1/2 pound smoked salmon, very thinly sliced
- Fresh dill sprigs, for garnish

Direction

- Stir together the yogurt, cucumber, lemon juice, olive oil, and dill in a small bowl to combine. Season with salt and pepper, to taste. Cover with plastic wrap and chill in the refrigerator until ready to use.
- Place the grated potatoes in a large dish towel and season with salt and pepper. Gather the ends and squeeze to wring out as much liquid as possible.
- Heat 1 tablespoon of vegetable oil in a large skillet over medium-high heat. Working in batches, drop spoonfuls of the potatoes into the pan, pressing gently with the back of a spoon to flatten. Cook for 2 to 3 minutes per side, until golden brown. Drain the latkes on paper towels. Continue cooking the latkes, adding more vegetable oil as needed.
- To assemble, top each latke with a dollop of yogurt sauce and a slice of smoked salmon. Garnish each latke stack with a sprig of dill.

72. Lemon Thyme Grilled Fish With Cucumbers And Arugula

Serving: Serves 4-6 | Prep: | Cook: | Ready in:

Ingredients

- 6 Halibut fillets. about 5 oz each
- Finely grated zest of 1 large lemon
- 2 tablespoons thyme leaves
- 1 tablespoon chopped parsley leaves, use a shap knife or scissors
- 3-4 medium-size cucumbers (about 1 pound in total)
- 1/2 teaspoon whole cumin
- 3/4 cup Greek yogurt (if you can't find any, use a very thick yogurt that has been hung in a cheesecloth for an hour)
- 1/2 teaspoon minced garlic
- 4 teaspoons lemon juice
- 1 teaspoon chopped dill
- 1/2 teaspoon coriander powder
- A pinch of cayenne pepper
- 1 tablespoon chopped mint
- 2 tablespoons olive oil
- 5 ounces baby arugula
- Salt and freshly ground pepper, to taste
- Drizzle of olive oil and fresh lemon juice to serve

Direction

- Season the fish with the grated lemon zest, thyme and parsley. Cover and refrigerate for 3-4 hours.
- Remove the fish 20 minutes before you start cooking to bring it to room temperature.
- Peel the cucumber, cut into 1-inch long sections and then cut into julienne strips. (Deseed the cucumbers if you prefer.) Toss with 1 teaspoon salt and let sit in a colander for 20 minutes.
- Toast the cumin seeds in a small pan over medium heat until they change color, 2-3 mins.
- Mix the cumin, garlic, lemon juice, dill, coriander powder and cayenne pepper into the yogurt.
- Pat the cucumbers dry with a paper towel and toss with the yogurt mixture. Season with salt and pepper and stir in the chopped mint.
- Prepare the grill (medium heat). Brush the fish with olive oil and season well with salt and pepper. Grill fish, turning once, until the fish is just cooked through, 6-8 minutes in total.
- Scatter the baby arugula leaves on the plate/s. Spoon the cucumbers over the leaves and

arrange the fish on the top. Season with a generous amount of lemon juice and a drizzle of good olive oil. Serve immediately.

- Do-ahead: You can prepare the yogurt mixture minus the cucumbers and mint ahead of time. Add the cucumbers and mint and season with salt and pepper just before serving.

73. Lentil And Vegetable Soup

Serving: Serves 8 | Prep: | Cook: | Ready in:

Ingredients

- 1 onion, diced
- 1 leek, sliced
- 4 cloves of garlic, peeled and chopped
- 2 teaspoons dried thyme
- 2 carrots, peeled and diced
- 6 mushrooms, diced or sliced
- 2 stalks of celery, diced
- 1 400g tin of chopped Italian tomatoes
- 1 cup French green lentils
- 60g rocket leaves
- 1/4 cup dill, chopped
- 1.5 litres of vegetable or meat stock
- 1 tablespoon olive oil

Direction

- Warm a large pot and add the olive oil, garlic, onion and leek and cook until the onion begins to turn translucent.
- Add the celery, carrot, thyme and mushrooms and cook for a few minutes until the carrot begins to soften.
- Then add the tinned tomatoes, lentils and stock and stir well. Cover and cook for 25 to 30 minutes. Season to taste.
- Before serving add the rocket and dill. Serve with warm crusty bread.

74. Light As Air Chickpea And Zucchini Fritters ~ Lemon, Herbs And Yogurt

Serving: Serves 10 | Prep: | Cook: | Ready in:

Ingredients

- 1 16 ounce can of chickpeas (also called garbanzo beans), rinsed and drained. I used lower sodium.
- 1 medium zucchini, grated. I use a box grater.
- 1 small fresh green or red tiny Thai pepper or jalapeno pepper, minced (optional).
- 2 lemons, zest half of one and place the zest in the bowl with the grated zucchini
- 1-2 garlic cloves, peeled and minced. I use a microplane zester for this. Add it to the bowl with the other ingredients.
- A generous hand full of fresh dill. About 1/4 cup. Or herb of your choice. Basil would be great.
- 1/3 - 1/2 cups cup Pamela's Gluten Free Baking Mix or self rising flour (see notes)
- 2 tablespoons milk
- 2 large eggs
- Sea salt or kosher salt to taste
- Olive oil for cooking. I used extra virgin unfiltered.
- Greek yogurt and lemon wedges for serving.

Direction

- Place the rinsed and drained chickpeas in the bowl of a food processor and whiz to a chunky consistency. Don't process the chickpeas all the way down as if you're making hummus. They should still have some structure. Place the zucchini, chili, garlic, lemon zest, dill, milk, salt and eggs in a large bowl. Add the processed chickpeas. Add Pamela's Gluten Free Baking Mix to the bowl and stir everything together. Start with 1/3 cup of Pamela's Gluten Free Mix and add more if the mixture seems too wet.
- Heat a large nonstick frying pan on medium high with a tablespoon or so of olive oil. I used

my nonstick Scanpan for this recipe. Drop batter by 1/3 cupful into the hot pan. Cook until golden brown on each side. Serve with lemon wedges and plain Greek yogurt. Makes about 10 fritters. Enjoy!

75. Low Fat & Healthy Red Potato Salad

Serving: Serves 10 | Prep: | Cook: | Ready in:

Ingredients

- 5 lb red potatoes, washed
- 1 1/2 cup low-fat mayonnaise
- 1 1/2 cup non-fat plain Greek yogurt
- 8 green onions, chopped
- 2 TBSP minced garlic
- 1 1/2 TBSP dill seed
- 1 TBSP celery seed
- ground black pepper & salt to taste

Direction

- Bring whole potatoes to a boil, sprinkle in a TBSP salt, and cook for 20 minutes. Stick a sharp knife in the largest one to test for doneness. Drain and set aside to cool.
- While potatoes are boiling mix the fat-free Greek yogurt, low-fat mayo, garlic, dill seed, celery seed, ground black pepper and salt into a medium mixing bowl and whisk till blended well.
- Cut the potatoes into large cubes (about 1 inch), and place in a large bowl. Pour the dressing over them and toss in the chopped green onion. Gently fold dressing and green onions into potatoes. Decorate with a pinch of green onions on top.
- VARIATION: This recipe is excellent with crumbled bacon--the full recipe will need one pound of cooked, drained and chopped bacon. Any leftover potato salad also makes a wonderful potato soup--just add evaporated

milk and simmer until hot--sprinkle with parmesan cheese.

76. Middle Eastern Zucchini Fritters

Serving: Makes 16 | Prep: | Cook: | Ready in:

Ingredients

- 500 grams zucchinis
- 3/4 teaspoon salt
- 200 grams carrots
- 3 scallions
- 1 small onion
- 3 tablespoons dill, chopped
- 4 tablespoons flat leaf parsley, chopped
- 100 grams feta cheese
- 140 grams flour
- 1 egg
- Freshly ground black pepper, to taste
- 1/4 teaspoon chili flakes
- Olive oil, for frying
- 200 grams Greek yoghurt

Direction

- Wash the zucchinis and finely grate. Put into a fine sieve, mix with 1/4 teaspoon salt and leave to drain for 20 minutes.
- Meanwhile, peel and finely grate the carrots. Squeeze out any excess moisture with your hands and put into a large bowl.
- Wash, trim, and finely chop the scallions. Add to the bowl.
- Peel and finely chop the onion and add to the bowl, followed by the chopped dill and parsley.
- Finely crumble the feta into the bowl.
- After 20 minutes, squeeze out any excess moisture from the zucchinis and add to the bowl. Then add the flour, egg, a bit of pepper, 1/4 teaspoon salt, and the chili flakes, and mix until everything is well incorporated.

- Pour enough olive oil into a pan so it covers the entire base. Heat the oil and test if the oil is hot enough by dropping in a tiny bit of batter—if it starts bubbling, you're good to go. For 4 fritters, drop 4 tablespoons of the zucchini mix into the pan. Flatten them slightly and fry on each side for 2 to 3 minutes. Remove from the pan and drain on a plate lined with kitchen paper. Proceed with the remaining batter.
- Just before serving, season the yoghurt with 1/4 teaspoon of salt and black pepper and serve each portion of zucchini fritters with a dollop of yoghurt.

77. Mild Cured Cucumbers

Serving: Makes makes | Prep: | Cook: | Ready in:

Ingredients

- 2000 grams cucumber
- 3 tablespoons ground black pepper
- 2 liters water
- 2 garlic young
- 2 dill inflorescence
- 2 horseradish leaves
- 2 tablespoons salt

Direction

- Wash the cucumbers and leave them in the water for 2-3 hours. This must be done, as this way the cucumbers will remain crispy and hard.
- While the cucumbers are being soaked, prepare a dish for curing. I used a common jar with a 3 liter capacity, however you can also use a ceramic dish or an enamel saucepan. Place a horseradish leaf and a dill inflorescence (you can take 2 or 3 for a dish with such a capacity) on the bottom of the jar, then add the cucumbers and garlic cloves among them.
- Prepare the brine - mix salt and ground pepper in a separate dish, then cover the mix boiling water, but do not boil the mixture. Thoroughly mix with a tablespoon until the salt is completely dissolved. Leave the brine to cool down a bit.
- When the brine is warm, carefully pour it into the jar with the cucumbers. Then cover with a lid and leave for 1-2 days. The prepared cucumbers should be stored in the fridge and if you're going on a picnic with your friends, place them into a plastic container with a lid.

78. Mom's Mushroom Barley Soup

Serving: Serves 10 to 12 hearty servings | Prep: | Cook: | Ready in:

Ingredients

- 2 tablespoons butter or canola oil (I prefer the flavor butter imparts)
- 2 cups diced yellow onions
- 2 cups diced carrots
- 2 cups diced celery
- 1 cup chopped leeks (white and light green parts only)
- 1 pound fresh white button mushrooms, half sliced, and half diced
- 8 cups chicken broth (low sodium) or chicken stock
- 1 mushroom bouillion cube, dissolved in 2 cups boiling water
- 1 cup pearl barley
- 1 teaspoon kosher salt, or more to taste
- freshly cracked black pepper to taste
- 1 tablespoon fresh chopped dill or 1 teaspoon dried dill leaves
- 2 tablespoons fresh Italian parsley leaves, chopped

Direction

- In a large soup pot sauté the onions, carrots, celery and leeks in the melted butter or oil over medium to medium high heat.
- Sauté for 10-12 minutes until the vegetables are soft and transparent, but not browned, adjusting heat as necessary.
- Clean the mushrooms by wiping them off with a damp paper towel before dicing and slicing. Add the mushrooms to the vegetables and cook for another 5-8 minutes.
- Stir the mushroom bouillon cube into the 2 cups boiling water. Add this with the 8 cups of broth to the soup pot. Bring to a boil, and then reduce to a simmer.
- Add the barley, dill, parsley, salt and pepper. Continue to simmer on low heat, with the pot partially covered, for one hour until the barley is tender.
- Check for seasoning. Serve in big bowls with a bit of chopped dill or parsley on top, and a hunk of bread for dunking. It is even better the next day!
- Note: The soup will thicken as it sits because the barley tends to absorb the broth. When reheating you may want to adjust the consistency by adding a small amount of water. This soup also freezes well.

79. Moroccan Squash With Vegetable Almond Pilaf

Serving: Serves 4 | Prep: | Cook: | Ready in:

Ingredients

- 1 cup dry couscous
- Pinch of saffron (optional)
- 2 small/medium Delicata Squash, cut in half lengthwise
- 3 medium parsnips, peeled and chopped into large pieces
- 4 medium carrots, peeled and chopped into large pieces
- 2 large red bell peppers, cut into large pieces
- 1 tablespoon Harissa Paste
- 2 teaspoons fresh ginger, grated
- 4 scallions, diced
- 2 tablespoons toasted sesame seeds (optional)
- 1/3 cup slivered almonds, toasted
- 1/4 cup fresh dill, chopped
- 1-2 teaspoons Za'atar
- 1-2 teaspoons Ras Al Hanout
- Salt, to taste
- Olive oil
- Toppings: Labneh (Lebanese strained yogurt) or Greek yogurt sprinkled with za'atar lemon or lime wedges Harissa paste drizzle of good olive oil

Direction

- Preheat the oven to 400F (375 if using convection roast). Line 1 large and 1 small rimmed baking sheet with parchment. (The red pepper takes less time to roast and needs its own baking sheet.)
- Brush the cut squash on both sides with olive oil. Sprinkle each cavity with salt, pepper, a sprinkle of Ras el Hanout and about ¼ tsp of fresh ginger. Place face down on the large baking sheet.
- Toss parsnips and carrots with olive oil, salt and pepper. Arrange in a single layer next to the squash. Toss the red pepper with olive oil and salt, place on the small baking sheet. The red pepper will roast for 12-15 min and the other vegetables need about 20-25 minutes, stirring them around halfway through the cooking process.
- While the vegetables are roasting, prepare the couscous (adding a pinch of saffron if using) according to package instructions (usually about 5 min) and toast the slivered almonds in a dry pan on the stovetop (3-5 min).
- Once the couscous is done, stir in some olive oil, 1 tsp za'atar, the diced scallions, toasted sesame seeds, almonds and fresh dill. Season with salt to taste.
- Once the vegetables are done, place the carrots, parsnips and red pepper in a bowl and

- toss with the remaining grated ginger and 1 Tbs Harissa.
- Fill the squash with couscous and a good helping of vegetables.
- Toppings should include: a side of Labneh or thick Greek yogurt sprinkled with za'atar and olive oil and side of Harissa paste. Lemons or lime wedges to squeeze on top.

80. Mushroom Stuffed Draniki

Serving: Makes 6 | Prep: | Cook: |Ready in:

Ingredients

- Mushroom Filling
- 1 ounce dried wild mushroom blend
- 1/4 cup minced red onion
- 1 teaspoon fresh dill
- salt & pepper
- For the Draniki
- 1 1/2 pounds potatoes, peeled
- 1/4 cup flour
- 1 egg
- 1/4 cup milk
- salt & pepper
- vegetable oil, for frying

Direction

- Rehydrate dried mushrooms according to package directions. Mince and add with onion to a pan with a little oil. Cook over medium heat until soft. Add dill and salt and pepper. Remove from pan and set aside
- Shred potatoes using a grater, food processor, or mandoline. Add remaining ingredients and stir together.
- Turn the oven on low. Heat about a 1/4 inch layer of oil in a large skillet over medium. Once oil sizzles when you drop a bit of potato in it, begin cooking. Spoon in draniki batter and flatten with a spoon.
- Add a small spoonful of the mushroom mixture. Top with more draniki batter.

- Cook until browned and no longer sticks to the bottom of the pan (this should take several minutes). Flip and cook on the other side. Hold in a warm oven while the rest of the drakini are cooked. Serve hot with sour cream.

81. My Classic Burger With Special Sauce

Serving: Makes 4 | Prep: | Cook: |Ready in:

Ingredients

- For the patties and to build the completed burger:
- Cheese mixture, see below
- 8 tablespoons (1 stick) cold unsalted butter, divided
- 1 pound 12 ounces ground beef (15 to 20% fat)
- 2 1/2 teaspoons kosher salt
- 1 teaspoon freshly ground pepper
- 4 soft burger buns
- Special sauce (see below)
- 4 small, inner iceberg lettuce leaves
- 4 tomato slices (fresh or roasted)
- crisp bacon slices, for topping
- 4 yellow onion slices
- thinly sliced dill pickles, for topping
- For the cheese and special sauce:
- 8 ounces cheese (I use a mix of Beecher's Sharp Cheddar and Fontina), cut into 1-inch chunks
- 1/4 cup plus 1/3 cup mayonnaise, divided
- 2 tablespoons dill relish
- 2 teaspoons yellow mustard
- 1 garlic clove
- 2 tablespoons ketchup
- 1/2 teaspoon soy sauce
- 1/2 teaspoon honey

Direction

- For the patties and to build the completed burger:

- Start by making the cheese mixture (see below for instructions).
- Grate 4 tablespoons of the cold butter and, in a large bowl, gently combine it with the beef, salt, and pepper. Refrigerate for at least one hour or overnight.
- When you are ready to cook your burgers, form the patties by gently gathering 4 ounces of beef into a ball and pressing it to create a patty. Sear the patties in a screaming hot cast-iron skillet for 3 minutes on one side. Flip, then continue to cook for 1 minute more before spooning a bit of the cheese mixture (see below for instructions) on top of the patty (or laying a slice of cheese if that is what you are using). Continue to cook for 1 to 2 minutes more, until the cheese is soft and the patty is cooked through. Set the patties aside to rest for a few minutes before building your burger.
- Note: For medium-rare, cook the burger to 130° F to 135° F; medium 140° F to 145° F; medium-well 150° F to 155° F; and well-done 160° F or higher.
- While the pan that you just cooked your burger in is still hot, add the rest of the butter and let it melt. Place four of the bun halves in the pan and toast until golden and crisp. Repeat until all the buns are toasted.
- Build your burger by slathering special sauce on BOTH sides of the bun. Add the patty and lettuce, tomatoes, bacon, onion, and LOTS of pickles. Top with the other crisped and sauce-smeared bun.
- For the cheese and special sauce:
- Combine the cheese and 1/4 cup mayonnaise in the bowl of a food processor and process until the cheese is cut up into tiny bits and the mixture is quite creamy. Refrigerate until ready to use. This mixture will keep for up to 2 weeks stored in an airtight container and refrigerated.
- Whisk the remaining 1/3 cup mayonnaise with the remaining ingredients (dill relish through honey). The burger sauce can be made up to 1 week in advance and stored, covered, in the refrigerator.

82. New England Seafood Chowder

Serving: Serves 6 | Prep: | Cook: |Ready in:

Ingredients

- 1 cup carrots, cut to match-sticks
- 1 cup leek, diced
- 1 cup waxy potatoes cut to match-sticks
- 1 cup russet potatoes cut to 1/4 inch dice
- 3/4 pound salmon filet, 1-inch pieces
- 3/4 pound cod filet, 1-inch pieces
- 1/2 pound shrimp, 1-inch pieces (can be whole, if small)
- 1/2 pound lobster meat, 1-inch pieces
- 3 cups seafood stock
- 2 cups whole milk
- 1 cup heavy cream
- 3 tablespoons fresh dill or parsley
- salt and pepper to taste
- olive oil

Direction

- In a large, heavy bottomed Dutch oven, heat the olive oil until smoking. Add the leeks and sauté until translucent, about 3-4 minutes. Add the carrots and sauté a few more minutes. Add both potato types, then the seafood stock. This should cover the vegetables. Cover with a lid and let simmer on low heat for 20-25 minutes, until the russet potatoes have disintegrated (this will help thicken the chowder) and the waxy potatoes and carrots are tender.
- Add the fish and shrimp and let simmer on very low for 5-8 minutes, until the fish is cooked through. At this point, avoid stirring much — or stir gently — as if you are rough with the chowder, all the fish will fall apart. Add the lobster meat.
- Add the milk and the cream and let come back to a gentle boil. Remove from the heat and taste. Add salt and pepper to taste. Finally, add your dill or parsley immediately before serving.

83. New Potato Salad With Crispy Radishes, Fennel & Celery

Serving: Serves 4 | Prep: | Cook: | Ready in:

Ingredients

- 1 pound baby potatoes
- 2 tablespoons apple cider vinegar or white wine vinegar
- 1 teaspoon Dijon mustard
- 3 tablespoons sunflower or safflower oil
- 1 cup medium red radishes, halved and thinly sliced (about 4 radishes)
- 1/2 cup medium celery ribs, thinly sliced crosswise on the diagonal (about 3 stalks)
- 1 small fennel bulb, halved, cored, and cut into bite-size pieces
- 1 pinch kosher salt and freshly ground pepper
- 2 tablespoons chopped dill

Direction

- In a large pot, cover the potatoes with water and bring to a boil over high heat. Reduce the heat to medium and simmer until tender, about 15 minutes. Drain and let cool.
- In a large bowl, whisk together the vinegar, mustard, and oil. Add the radishes, celery, and fennel. Slice the potatoes into rounds (removing the peel if you prefer) and add to the bowl. Stir together and season the salad with salt and pepper. Fold in the dill. Serve immediately or refrigerate for up to 1 day.

84. No Mayo New Potato Salad With Lemon, Dill, And Chives

Serving: Serves 4 | Prep: 0hours0mins | Cook: 0hours0mins | Ready in:

Ingredients

- 1 1/2 pounds small red new potatoes, quartered
- 1 celery stalk
- 2 radishes
- 2 tablespoons extra-virgin olive oil
- 3 tablespoons plain Greek yogur
- 2 tablespoons fresh-squeezed lemon juice
- 1/4 teaspoon Dijon mustard
- 1 tablespoon fresh minced chives
- 1 tablespoon fresh minced baby dill
- Ground pepper, to taste

Direction

- Boil quartered potatoes for about 10 minutes. You don't want them too soft. Remove the potatoes from heat, drain, and rinse in cold water. Add to a bowl, cover, and refrigerate until ready to make the salad.
- Meanwhile, finely dice the celery and radishes, either by hand or in a food processor.
- In a small bowl, whisk together the oil, yogurt, lemon juice, Dijon mustard, minced chives, minced dill, and ground black pepper, to taste. Take a taste to see if it needs more of any one flavor.
- Stir into the bowl of potatoes, then cover and refrigerate to let flavors meld until ready to serve.

85. Pashteda (Mushroom Pie)

Serving: Serves 8-10 | Prep: | Cook: | Ready in:

Ingredients

- Ingredients for the crust:
- • 2 ½ cups all purpose flour
- • 2 sticks cold butter
- • 1 cup sour cream
- • 1 teaspoon baking powder
- • 1 teaspoon baking soda
- • ½ teaspoon salt

- Ingredients for the mushroom filling:
- • 2 pounds fresh mushrooms (any kind you like or a variety of 2-3)
- • 2 medium onions (diced)
- • 3 tablespoons olive oil
- • 2 tablespoons dry mushroom soup (I prefer (OSEM) instant soup & seasoning mix
- • 2 eggs
- • 1 cup of each shredded cheese (Gruyere and Cheddar)
- • 2 tablespoon fresh parsley
- • 1 tablespoon fresh dill

Direction

- Put in a mixing bowl the flour, salt baking powder and baking soda. Mix until well combined. Add butter, precut in small pieces and with a knife or pastry cutter, work in the butter. You should see bits of butter thru the mixture. Add the sour cream and gather the dough together. Press in ¾ of the dough to an 8 by 8 casserole or glass baking dish with tall sides. The remaining ¼ of the dough (covered in plastic), and the baking dish with the crust, refrigerate until the filling is ready.
- In a large skillet sauté the onions until soft and lightly browned. Add mushrooms (each cut lengthwise) and continue to sauté on a medium flame until soft and browned. In one cup of boiling water dissolve the dry mushroom soup and pour in to the skillet. Continue cooking until the liquid is completely evaporated. Transfer to a bowl, taste for seasoning, add parsley and dill, and let it cool for a few minutes before adding the eggs. Mix in the eggs (lightly beaten).
- To assemble the pie, take out the chilled baking dish with the dough from refrigerator. Spread the mushroom filling, sprinkle the chesses on top. Roll out the remaining ¼ of the dough, cut it in strips and orange them on the top of the pie in a pattern you like. Some time I shred the cold dough on a large side of the grader. Bake in a 350 degrees preheated oven for about 40-45 minutes. Serve hot or room temperature.

86. Pressure Cooker Corned Beef Brisket With Charred Cabbage And Dill Vinaigrette

Serving: Serves 6 | Prep: 0hours0mins | Cook: 0hours0mins | Ready in:

Ingredients

- 2 cups apple juice
- 2 tablespoons maple syrup
- 1 teaspoon Instacure #1
- 1 teaspoon yellow mustard seeds
- 1/2 teaspoon tellicherry black peppercorns
- 1/2 teaspoon allspice berries
- 1/2 teaspoon caraway seesds
- 4 bay leaves
- 1/2 cup kosher salt
- 1 quart ice
- 4 pounds cut of beef brisket
- 2 tablespoons canola oil
- 2 medium-sized yellow onions, peeled and halved
- 2 carrots, cut into 1-inch pieces
- 2 tablespoons brown miso
- 4 cloves of garlic
- 2 tablespoons unsalted butter
- 1 tablespoon Dijon mustard
- 1 shallot, peeled and minced
- 1/2 cup extra virgin olive oil
- 3 tablespoons red wine vinegar
- 1/4 teaspoon fine sea salt
- Freshly ground black pepper
- 1/4 cup fresh dill, chopped
- Half a head of green cabbage

Direction

- Place 1 1/2 quarts of cold water and the apple juice in a large pot and bring to a boil. Add the maple syrup, Instacure, mustard seed, peppercorn, allspice, caraway seed, bay leaves, and salt. Cook for 3 minutes at a rapid boil,

then turn off the heat. Add the ice and wait for the brine to lower to room temperature.
- Place the brisket in a large tub and cover with the brine. Cover and place in the refrigerator.
- After 1 week, pull the brisket out of the brine and strain the brine. Save the spices and bay and discard the liquid.
- In a large skillet, warm 1 tablespoon of the canola oil over medium-high heat. Add the onions to the pan and cook for 15 minutes, turning once in a while, until well browned and a touch charred. Set aside.
- Place the pressure cooker on the stove, lid removed. Place the brisket in the pot, add the charred onions, carrots, miso, whole garlic cloves, 1 tablespoon of the butter, and the strained spices. Cover by 2 inches with room temperature water. Lock the lid in place and set the pressure cooker to meat. Set the time for 55 minutes.
- In the midst of the pressure cookery, make the vinaigrette and char the cabbage. In a mason jar, combine the mustard, shallot, olive oil, red wine vinegar, sea salt, pepper, and dill. Cap with a lid and shake vigorously. Set aside.
- Place a large skillet over medium-high heat and add the remaining tablespoons of canola oil and butter. Cut the half head of cabbage into six wedges and when the butter has begun to bubble and froth, place each cabbage wedge in the pan. Season with a pinch of salt. Char for 10 minutes, then, using tongs, turn each wedge over and char for 5 more minutes. When done, remove the pan from heat and set aside.
- Check the brisket and make sure it's really tender. A paring knife should plunge into the meat with little resistance. If it's tough, cook longer. If it's tender, remove the brisket, let it rest for 10 minutes on a sheet pan and then slice it against the grain into 1/2-inch thick slices.
- Place 2 slices of brisket on each of six plates, then top each with a charred cabbage wedge. Circle each plate with a tablespoon or two of re-shaken dill vinaigrette.

87. Purple Carrot Meze (Tarator)

Serving: Serves 4-6 | Prep: | Cook: | Ready in:

Ingredients

- 3-4   purple carrots
- 1-2   Cloves of Garlic
- 1 cup Turkish Yogurt
- 1/5 bunch dill (or parsley)
- salt & pepper

Direction

- Grate purple carrots. Place them in a pot add 1/5 glass of water. On low heat simmer without lid for 5-6 minutes until they are soft.
- Place them in a bowl and let them cool. Add grated garlic, salt and pepper to the yogurt. Mix in the purple carrots. Chill before serving. Drizzle olive oil on top and garnish with dill or parsley.

88. Quick Pickles

Serving: Makes pickles from two cucumbers | Prep: | Cook: | Ready in:

Ingredients

- 1 cup distilled white vinegar
- 2 tablespoons granulated sugar
- 4 tablespoons water
- 1 1/2 teaspoons kosher salt
- 1 teaspoon dry dill weed
- 2 cloves of garlic, lightly smashed
- 1   whole Thai bird chili pepper
- 2   bay leaves
- 2   cucumbers, cut into thick slices

Direction

- Begin by adding the vinegar, water, sugar, salt, garlic, and chili pepper to a sauce pan and

bring to a boil, stirring well to mix in the sugar. My kids cannot stand the smell of cooking vinegar, and I do it quite a bit with Asian dipping sauces, however I think they are now getting used to it! Once boiling, remove from the heat, and add the dill weed. Let the pickling mixture completely cool. Add in the bay leaves.
- To a clean mason jar, add the cut cucumbers, arranging them the best you can. Pour in the cooled mixture, cover, and let sit in the refrigerator for at least 4 hours, however overnight is probably best. When you are ready, open and serve. Now you have pickles any day of the week, and is probably much more affordable than getting them at your local market.
- These are good in the refrigerator for a couple of weeks, then they get pretty soft. They typically do not last that long in the refrigerator though.

89. Quinoa "Fried Rice"

Serving: Serves 6 | Prep: | Cook: | Ready in:

Ingredients

- 1/4 pound Sweet Pork Sausage, casings removed
- 4 cups Quinoa, cooked
- Extra Virgin Olive Oil
- 6 pieces Farm Eggs
- 3 cups Arugula, chopped
- 1/4 cup Dill, chopped
- 3 pieces Persian Cucumber, diced
- Sriracha for serving, optional

Direction

- Put a cast iron pan on the stove top on medium high heat and cook your pork sausage, breaking it up as you go. When cooked, remove from pan with a slotted spoon and place into a mixing bowl.
- Toast cooked quinoa in the rendered fat from the sausage so that the quinoa gets a little crispy. Season with salt and pepper to taste and add quinoa to mixing bowl. (Note: If you have just cooked your quinoa before doing this, allow it to cool first so that it doesn't just absorb the fat and become mushy)
- Lower the temperature of the pan to medium low. Add some extra virgin olive oil to the pan just to coat the bottom and crack your six eggs into the pan. Season the eggs with salt & pepper. Let the eggs cook for a minute as if you were to make sunny side up eggs, then crack the yolks and begin to move the eggs around in the pan so that you get a scramble that shows both the white and yellow of the egg. Cook to your liking (soft and fluffy or uber crispy!) Add your eggs to your mixing bowl
- Add arugula, dill, and cucumbers to your bowl. Drizzle the ingredients with extra virgin olive oil and sprinkle with salt and pepper. Toss ingredients to combine. Taste and adjust seasoning/oil if necessary. Serve with Sriracha on the side. For fun, try serving out of Chinese takeout containers!

90. Quinoa And Farro Salad With Pickled Fennel

Serving: Serves 6 to 8 as a side dish | Prep: | Cook: | Ready in:

Ingredients

- For the Pickled Fennel:
- 1 medium fennel bulb, fronds removed but with stems trimmed, quartered and sliced lengthwise into 1/8-inch planks
- 1 hot dried chili (optional)
- 2 sprigs dill
- 1/2 teaspoon yellow mustard seeds
- 1/2 teaspoon fennel seeds
- 1/4 cup sugar

- 1 tablespoon kosher salt
- 3/4 cup apple cider vinegar
- 3/4 cup water
- For the Salad:
- 1 1/2 cups cooked and cooled farro
- 1 1/2 cups cooked and cooled quinoa
- 3 tablespoons olive oil
- 1/2 cup finely (1/4-inch) chopped pickled fennel
- 1 tablespoon fennel pickling liquid
- Salt and freshly ground black pepper to taste
- 1/4 cup roughly chopped dill leaves (or half dill, half fennel fronds if you saved them)

Direction

- For the Pickled Fennel:
- Put the fennel in a 1-quart jar. Add the chili (if using), dill, mustard and fennel seeds.
- In a small saucepan, combine the sugar, salt, vinegar and water. Bring to a boil over high heat and then pour into the jar with the fennel. Screw on the lid and refrigerate and serve once cool. The pickled fennel will keep in the fridge for at least 2 weeks.
- For the Salad:
- In a serving bowl, combine all of the ingredients and fold gently to combine. Taste and add more salt and pepper, pickling juices or olive oil if you'd like. Serve right away or let the salad sit at room temperature for up to an hour before serving. It will also keep in the fridge for a couple of days.

91. Radish & Cucumber Salad

Serving: Serves 4 | Prep: | Cook: | Ready in:

Ingredients

- 12 ounces radishes, cut in half lengthwise and thinly sliced
- 2/3 English cucumber, peeled, cut in half lengthwise, and thinly sliced
- 2/3 cup sliced green onions
- 1 tablespoon minced fresh dill, optional
- 1/2 cup sour cream
- couple pinches Kosher salt
- couple pinches freshly ground black pepper

Direction

- Toss together the radishes, cucumber, green onions, dill, if desired, and sour cream in a large bowl.
- Season to taste with salt and pepper.
- Transfer to a serving bowl and serve immediately.

92. Radish Canapés

Serving: Makes 30 | Prep: | Cook: | Ready in:

Ingredients

- For the crackers
- • 1 cup all-purpose flour
- • 1/2 cup butter, room temperature
- • 4 ounces Gruyere cheese, grated
- • 4 ounces Italian Capicolla ham, diced
- • 2 teaspoons fresh thyme leaves
- • Ground black pepper and 1/2 teaspoon coarse salt
- For the cheese mousse:
- • 12 Spreadable Cheese Wedges (garlic& herb flavor), room temperature
- • Kosher salt and freshly ground black pepper to taste
- • 2 teaspoons fresh thyme leaves plus more for garnish
- • 1/3 cup heavy cream, whipped to soft peaks
- • Radishes, turnips and cucumber thin half-moon slices
- For the Taramosalata canapés
- • 30 slices Cocktail Rye or Pumpernickel bread, lightly toasted and cooled
- • 1 cup of the Taramosalata caviar
- • 1 tablespoon lemon zest
- • 1 tablespoon lemon juice
- • 1 tablespoon fresh dill, finely chopped

- 2 whole green onions, thinly sliced
- 1/2 teaspoon freshly ground black pepper
- 1 bunch fresh radishes, very thinly sliced into rounds
- Chives or green part of spring onions, dill sprigs and Kalamata petted olives for garnish

Direction

- For the crackers
- To make the crackers: Preheat the oven to 375 degrees. Line a baking sheet with parchment paper. Place the flour, butter, cheese, a pinch of salt and a few grinds of black pepper in the bowl of a food processor. Process until the dough just comes together and starts to form a ball.
- Dump the dough onto a lightly floured surface; add the diced ham and thyme; knead a few times to pull the dough together. Roll the dough into a log about 1- inch thick and 14-inches long. Wrap in plastic and chill at list for 1 hour. The can be made 1 day ahead.
- With a knife or dough scraper, cut the dough log into 1/4-inch rounds. Bake the crackers for 15-20 minutes, until they are light golden brown on the bottom. Let cool on the baking sheet for at least 10 minutes; then remove to a wire rack to cool to room temperature.
- To make the mousse: In a food processor, puree the cheese wedges until very smooth; transfer to a mixing bowl; fold in thyme; season with salt and pepper, to taste. Fold the whipped cream into the mousse until well blended. There should be no lumps.
- Transfer the mousse to a pastry bag fitted with a round tip. Pipe the mousse onto the crackers and garnish each with radish and cucumber slices. Arrange on a serving platter, garnish with turnip, cucumber and radish rounds, sprinkle with thyme leaves. Serve.
- For the Taramosalata canapés
- In a mixing bowl combine Taramosalata, lemon zest and juice, chopped dill, green onions and pepper. Whisk until everything is incorporated and the spread is smooth. Spread 1 heaping teaspoon over the tops of cooled toasts. Arrange 3 radish slices in any pattern you like; garnish with chives and dill sprigs. Transfer to serving platter and scatter the Kalamata olives around the platter. Serve.

93. Rainbow Gazpacho

Serving: Serves half a gallon of soup | Prep: | Cook: | Ready in:

Ingredients

- 4 good-sized heirloom tomatoes, cored and cut into large chunks
- 1 yellow bell pepper, cored, seeded and cut into large chunks
- 1 orange bell pepper, cored, seeded and cut into large chunks
- 1 large red onion, peeled and cut into large chunks
- 1 English cucumber, seeded and cut into large chunks
- 4 cloves of garlic, peeled
- 1/2 cup fresh dill
- one 46 ounces bottle of low-salt vegetable juice, such as low-salt V8 or low-salt 365 "Vital Veggie"
- 1/4 cup best quality olive oil
- 1/4 cup apple cider vinegar
- juice of one Meyer lemon (or any lemon)
- kosher salt and ground pepper (optional)

Direction

- Using a food processor, chop first the tomatoes, then the peppers, next the cucumber and finally the onion. Combine all the chopped vegetables in a large, non-reactive bowl.
- Next, chop the garlic and fresh dill in the processor. Add to vegetables.
- Pour in the vegetable juice and stir to combine.
- Add the olive oil, vinegar, lemon juice and mix in well. Taste and adjust seasoning.
- Chill several hours before serving.

94. Rassolnik, Traditional Russian Soup With Pickles

Serving: Serves 4 | Prep: | Cook: | Ready in:

Ingredients

- • 1 tablespoon any neutral oil
- • 1 pound beef or veal stew meat, cut in bite size pieces + a couple pieces of meat on the bone
- • 1 yelow onion, finely chopped
- • 2 garlic cloves, crushed
- • 1 teaspoon Herbs De Provence, rubbed in palms of your hands
- • 1/2 teaspoon red pepper flakes
- • 6-7 cups water, depending how thick or thin you like your soup
- • Kosher salt to taste
- • 1/3 cup pearled barley, rinsed and drained
- • 2 medium Russet potatoes, peeled and cut into 1/4- inches cubes
- • 1 medium carrot, peeled and shredded
- • 1 parsley root or parsnip, peeled and shredded
- • 2 celery ribs, peeled and thinly sliced
- • 1 large meaty tomato, peeled, seeded and finely chopped
- • About 4 medium pickles (preferably crunchy Kosher Dill Pickles in brine) peeled and finely chopped
- • Pickling brine to taste
- • Chopped fresh parsley and dill for garnish

Direction

- Heat the oil in a large saucepan or Dutch oven over high heat. Add the meat and cook, stirring often, until browned. Transfer to a plate.
- Add the onion and cook on medium, stirring occasionally until soft and translucent. Add the shredded carrots, parsley root or parsnips, celery, garlic and Herbs De Provence and red pepper flakes; cook, stirring, until soft and fragrant.
- Return the meat; add water, about 1 1/2 teaspoons of salt and barley. Bring to a boil; skim the surface with a large spoon to remove any scum. Reduce heat to low and simmer, partially covered, for 1 hour. Then add potatoes and continue cooking until the meat and potatoes are tender, for about 1/2 an hour to 45 minutes more.
- Add the tomato and pickles; cook for about 5 minutes. Now will be a good time to taste and add whatever seasonings you fill are needed. If the soup needs salt, add about 1/4 cup of the Pickling brine and then taste again; add some more if needed.
- To serve, ladle the hot soup into bowls, garnish with chopped fresh parsley and dill. It is also traditional to serve Rassolnik with a dollop of sour cream. Enjoy.

95. Red Chard With Festive Spices

Serving: Serves 4 as a side dish | Prep: 0hours0mins | Cook: 0hours0mins | Ready in:

Ingredients

- 1 large bunch of red-veined Swiss Chard
- 1/2 teaspoon caraway seeds
- 1 tablespoon olive oil
- 1 tablespoon butter
- 1 small onion, diced
- 2 ribs celery, diced
- 1/4 cup sherry (or white wine)
- 1/3 cup heavy cream
- 1/3 cup sour cream
- 1.5 tablespoons dried dill
- 1/8 teaspoon (scant) freshly grated nutmeg

Direction

- Prepare the chard by washing and drying it well. Then strip the leaves from the tough stems and chop them roughly. Dice the stems and reserve.

- In a heavy bottomed pan with a lid over medium-high heat, toast the caraway seeds in olive oil until fragrant, about one minute.
- Add the butter to the pan, and when it's melted, sauté the onion, celery, and chard stems with a pinch of salt and pepper until soft and translucent (but not brown), 5 to 7 minutes.
- Deglaze the pan with sherry and add the chard leaves, tossing to coat. Cover the pan and wilt the chard leaves, about 5 minutes.
- Whip together the cream, sour cream, and dill with a big pinch of salt and a few grinds of fresh cracked black pepper. When the chard has begun to wilt, stir in your cream mixture and reduce the heat to low. Grate the fresh nutmeg over your greens, and warm through, about 2 to 3 minutes.

96. Red, White, And Blue Flannel Hash

Serving: Serves 2 | Prep: | Cook: | Ready in:

Ingredients

- 3 medium-large beets, scrubbed and trimmed
- 3/4 pound small blue-skinned potatoes (can substitute 2 large russets), diced
- 1 medium Vidalia onion
- 1 1/2 tablespoons chopped fresh dill
- 1/2 - 1 cups turkey scraps, roughly chopped
- 1 egg

Direction

- Preheat the oven to 400 degrees.
- Arrange the beets in a small baking dish and fill with enough water to submerge the beets 1 inch. Season with salt, cover the dish with foil, and bake in the oven for 30-40 minutes, until the beets are fork tender. Allow beets to cool enough to handle. Remove skins with a paring knife — they should come off easily. Dice beets and set aside in a medium mixing bowl.
- In the meantime, while the beets are roasting, coat a large skillet with olive oil and sauté the potatoes over medium-high heat. When the potatoes are tender, but not completely cooked, add the onions and season generously with salt and pepper. Continue to sauté until the onions and potatoes are slightly caramelized, another 5-7 minutes. Add the potato-onion mixture to the beets and allow both to cool. In a small cup or bowl, scramble 1 of the eggs. Add to the beet-potato mixture along with the turkey, dill and ½ teaspoon of salt. Toss until the vegetables and turkey are fully coated.
- With a paper towel, remove any scraps from the skillet so it is more or less clean, and add another generous coating of olive oil. Get the oil nice and hot, then add the hash in one layer, pressing down with your spatula to form a large cake. Cook for a few minutes until the bottom is crispy and the hash has firmed up. Flip in sections and cook until the other side is crispy. Remove the hash and split between two serving plates. Top with a fried egg and serve immediately.

97. Rice, Dill And Olive Filled Tomatoes

Serving: Makes 5 stuffed tomatoes | Prep: 0hours0mins | Cook: 0hours0mins | Ready in:

Ingredients

- 5 nice round tomatoes, about 4 inches in diameter
- 3 tablespoons olive oil
- 1/2 cup finely diced onion
- 1 clove minced garlic
- 1/2 cup tomato pulp
- 1/2 teaspoon salt
- 1 cup long grain white rice

- 1 1/2 cups vegetable broth
- 1/2 cup minced fresh dill
- 1/4 cup chopped Kalamata olives
- Salt and pepper for seasoning the rice

Direction

- Slice each tomato about 1/4 of the way down, saving the tops. Seed each tomato with your clean hands and scoop out the pulp to create nice little bowls. Reserve about 1/2 cup of the pulp and chop it finely.
- Place the tomatoes and the tops cut side down on paper toweling while you prepare the rice filling.
- In a medium sauce pan heat the oil and add the onion and garlic. Sauté until the vegetables soften and become fragrant. Stir in the rice and then add the tomato pulp and 1/2 teaspoon of salt. Cook over medium heat for just a minute.
- Add the vegetable broth and bring the mixture up to a simmer and continue to simmer, covered until the rice absorbs the liquid. (15 to 20 minutes). Cool the mixture to room temperature.
- Once cooled, stir the dill and olives into the rice and then taste for seasoning. Add salt and pepper as needed.
- Place the tomatoes into a shallow baking dish and then fill each with the rice mixture. They each should be a little overflowing. Place the tomato tops over and then bake in a pre-heated 350F oven for 30 to 40 minutes. Serve warm or at room temperature.

98. Roast Carrots With A Few Pals

Serving: Serves 2-4 | Prep: | Cook: |Ready in:

Ingredients

- 4 organic carrots, peeled
- 1 parsnip, peeled
- 1 golden beet, peeled
- 1 yellow pepper, sliced and de-seeded
- 1 Spanish or Vidalia onion, peeled and quartered
- 6 cloves of garlic, whole
- 1 Meyer lemon, quartered
- 1 teaspoon ground sumac
- 1/2 teaspoon Aleppo pepper
- sprinkle of sea salt
- 1/4 teaspoon fresh milled pepper
- olive oil
- Meyer lemon wedges
- dill for garnish

Direction

- Cut the carrots and parsnip into 4 inch lengths. Then quarter lengthwise. Slice the beets and quarter the onion. Preheat the oven to 375 degrees.
- Coat the bottom of a large shallow pan with olive oil. Arrange all the vegetables and lemon in the pan in a single layer. Sprinkle the salt, pepper, and spice on top. Turn the veggies over and around to coat with oil on all sides.
- Bake in the oven for about 50 minutes until browned on the outside and cooked through. Midway turn the veggies over. Serve as a side. Squeeze lemon juice on top and garnish with fresh dill. Brown rice and teff cooked in carrot juice are featured with these roasted veggies.

99. Roasted Asparagus Soup With Lovage & Dill

Serving: Makes 7 cups | Prep: | Cook: |Ready in:

Ingredients

- 1 tablespoon olive oil
- 3/4 pound green asparagus, trimmed
- 3/4 pound white asparagus, trimmed
- 3 tablespoons butter
- 1/2 cup thinly sliced shallot
- 1 1/2 cups peeled and diced new potatoes
- 3 tablespoons chopped lovage (or celery leaves if lovage is not available)

- 6 cups chicken broth
- 3/4 cup chopped fresh dill
- Salt and white pepper, to taste
- Sour cream, for garnish (optional)

Direction

- Heat the oven to 400° F. Rub the asparagus with the olive oil and roast for 20 minutes. Let cool a bit, then cut into 2-inch pieces.
- In a large pot, melt the butter and cook the shallots at low heat, until soft.
- Stir in the potatoes, lovage, and broth. Turn up the heat, bring to a boil, then simmer until the potatoes are tender, about 8 minutes.
- Remove from the heat and stir in the dill and asparagus.
- Process in a food processor or blender, in batches, until smooth.
- Season to taste with the salt and white pepper. Garnish each serving with a dollop of sour cream, if desired.

100. Roasted Cauliflower Buttermilk Soup

Serving: Serves 4-6 | Prep: | Cook: | Ready in:

Ingredients

- 1 med head cauliflower, cut into florets
- 1 med onion, rough chopped
- 3 cloves of garlic, minced
- 3 small red potatoes, cubed
- 1 teaspoon dried dill
- 1/2 teaspoon paprika
- 1 tablespoon butter
- 3 ounces large handfulls baby spinach
- 4 cups chicken stock
- 1 cup buttermilk
- 1 cup white cheddar, shredded

Direction

- Preheat oven to 450. Combine the first 6 ingredients in a roasting pan with some olive oil and season with salt and pepper. Roast in the top third of the oven for about 40 minutes or until a nice golden brown color is achieved.
- In a large pot melt the butter on medium heat and sauté the spinach until wilted. Add the roasted vegetables and stir until well mixed. Add the chicken stock, bring to a simmer then reduce heat to low, cover and cook for 20-30 minutes.
- After the vegetables are tender remove from heat and use an immersion blender to roughly puree soup (I like to leave it a chunky texture, but you could puree it smooth if you prefer). Blend in the buttermilk and shredded cheese then season to taste with salt and pepper (and more dill if you like). Enjoy!

101. Romanian Creamed Chicken (Ciulama De Pui)

Serving: Serves 8 generously | Prep: | Cook: | Ready in:

Ingredients

- 1 large chicken, cleaned, skinned, and cut into 8 pieces
- 4-6 additional legs, skinned and thighs separated
- 1 large yellow cooking onion, diced
- 4 large cloves garlic, minced
- 2-3 ribs celery, diced
- 2 large carrots, peeled and diced
- 1 pound cremini mushrooms, wiped clean and sliced
- 2 tablespoons unbleached all-purpose flour
- 2 cups 35% or 18% cream, or a combination
- 1 tablespoon sweet paprika
- sea salt and freshly cracked black pepper, to taste
- fresh parsley or dill, chopped

Direction

- Preheat oven to 325°F. In a large bowl, mix together onions, garlic, celery, and carrots. Place half the vegetable mixture in an ovenproof lidded casserole. Layer chicken pieces (including neck and gizzards, if using) on top and cover with remaining vegetable mixture. Cover casserole and bake for 1 hour.
- Meanwhile, cook mushrooms in a pan or skillet over medium-high heat, stirring frequently until they begin to give up their moisture. When all their liquid has been released and they begin to brown slightly, remove them from the heat and reserve. (Cooking them separately means they don't water down the stew.)
- After 1 hour of cooking time, remove casserole from oven and check stew. The vegetables should be nearly cooked through, the chicken should be starting to brown, and there should be a nice amount of liquid in the pot. (If vegetables are still crisp and chicken is undercooked, cover casserole and return to oven for an additional 15–20 minutes.) Place flour in a mixing bowl and add cream while whisking constantly until the mixture is smooth. Add cream, reserved mushrooms, and paprika to stew. Cover casserole and return to oven for 1/2 hour.
- Remove casserole from oven and stir contents. Season with salt and pepper to taste. Sprinkle with chopped fresh parsley or dill before serving with mamaliga and/or fresh bread.

102. Rounds, Roots And Shoots: A Vernal Salad

Serving: Serves 4-6 | Prep: | Cook: | Ready in:

Ingredients

- Salad
- 8-10 Baby New Potatoes
- 10-12 Fresh Asparagus Stalks
- 1 Zucchini
- 3-4 Spring Onions
- 1/2 cup Dill, chopped
- 1 cup Marcona Almonds
- 1/2 cup Microgreens
- Dressing
- 1 Clove of Garlic
- 1 teaspoon Dijon
- 1 tablespoon Mayo, or vegan substitute
- 2-3 tablespoons Extra Virgin Olive Oil
- 1 Lemon, juiced
- 1 tablespoon Apple Cider Vinegar
- A dusting of Red Pepper
- Salt & Pepper to taste

Direction

- Bring a pot of salted water to a boil. Add the potatoes and cook about 15-20 minutes, until a fork easily slides through the middle. Meanwhile, if you have a double cooker or a steamer, put that on top of the boiling potatoes and blanch the asparagus for a 3-4 minutes only. Otherwise you can drop them into boiling water for 2-3 minutes. Rinse the asparagus immediately with cold water and place in a bowl of ice water. When the potatoes are done, drain and put them in a bowl of ice water too.
- Slice the zucchini thin and cut the rounds into quarters, so they are mini bite-size. Slice the spring onions all the way up into the green. Add the zucchini, spring onions, almonds and dill to a salad bowl and set aside.
- Mix up the dressing by mincing the garlic. I always make my dressings in a jar because with a lid on tight, you can really give it a good shake and prove to the world that even oil and vinegar can sometimes mix. So put your garlic into a small jar with the juice of half the lemon and the rest of the ingredients. Shake until it is creamy. Taste and adjust seasonings.
- Drain and dry the potatoes and asparagus and cut into small bite size pieces. Toss together with the zucchini, spring onions and dill. Give the dressing a good vigorous blend and pour onto the salad. Taste and adjust. I found mine

needed the juice of the entire lemon. Serve on a bed of lettuce with a carefree sprinkling of micro greens.

- Options: Chopped, hard-boiled egg; avocado slices; sun-dried tomatoes for that bit of sour; sunflower seeds for added crunch; garden-fresh snap peas for even more sweet green; basil, cilantro, or mint for more savory zing. This salad is really happy company to just about any of springs edible delights so let your garden or your local farmer inspire your whims.

103. Salmon Soup With Mushrooms, Broccoli, Spinach And Corn

Serving: Makes 2 servings | Prep: | Cook: | Ready in:

Ingredients

- 400 grams raw salmon fillet
- 200 grams smoked salmon fillet
- 10-15 brown mushrooms
- 3 handfuls of spinach
- 1 broccoli
- 1 corn
- onion, garlic, dill, salt, ground pepper
- white wine (optional)

Direction

- Initially chop the mushrooms and let them soak in a bowl of warm water for half an hour. While the mushrooms do their thing, sauté the chopped onion and garlic and then add the raw salmon in pieces. Pour some white wine and when the alcohol evaporates, add -the colored now- water in which the mushrooms soaked.
- Add the corn in pieces, season with salt and ground pepper and let it boil for 10 minutes.
- Then add the broccoli tassels, mushrooms, spinach and dill in this order and with a difference of 2-3 minutes each ingredients

from the next one. Your goal is to have your vegetables cooked, but still vibrant green as they keep most of their nutrients like that.

104. Salt And Vinegar Potato Salad {vegan}

Serving: Serves 8-10 | Prep: | Cook: | Ready in:

Ingredients

- 12 medium yukon gold potatoes (or any kind you like!), scrubbed and cut into 1-inch chunks
- 1/4 cup white vinegar, plus more to taste
- 1/3 cup olive oil, plus more to taste
- 1 bunch green onions, thinly sliced
- 1/4 cup chopped fresh dill
- 1/4 cup chopped fresh parsley
- 1 stalk celery, finely chopped (omit if you're not into celery)
- salt and pepper, to taste

Direction

- Add the potatoes to a large pot of salted water. Cover, and bring to a boil. When the water boils, remove the lid and let the potatoes boil for 10-15 minutes until fork tender but not falling apart.
- Drain the potatoes, and transfer to a large bowl. Let cool for about 10 minutes until not hot but still slightly warm.
- Transfer the potatoes to a bowl, and add the olive oil, vinegar, onions, dill, parsley, and celery. Stir together, sprinkle with salt and pepper.
- Taste, and adjust seasonings to your preference - remember that potatoes absorb salt, so add more right before serving if you think it needs it. Add more vinegar if you'd like a tangier salad, or more oil if the potatoes seem dry.
- Serve slightly warm, at room temperature, or chilled. Can be made up to 3 days in advance and kept in the fridge.

105. Sardine Tartine

Serving: Serves 1 | Prep: | Cook: |Ready in:

Ingredients

- 1 4.25 oz package of quality Portuguese sardines in olive oil (I prefer the Bela brand)
- 3-5 cucumber slices
- Ricotta cheese for spreading
- Shallot or red onion, thinly sliced
- Dill sprigs, cracked red pepper flakes, and sea salt for garnish
- 1 -2 slices whole rye bread

Direction

- Lightly toast the rye bread. Then, spread on a generous amount of ricotta cheese. Layer the cucumber and shallot slices on top. Next, spread the sardines evenly over the cucumber and shallot slices. Sprinkle with cracked red pepper and sea salt. Finish with a sprig of dill. That's it!

106. Schnitzel With German Cucumber Salad

Serving: Serves 2 | Prep: 0hours20mins | Cook: 0hours10mins |Ready in:

Ingredients

- Chicken Schnitzel
- 2 Organic Chicken Breasts (Skinless & Boneless)
- 1 teaspoon Salt
- 1/2 tablespoon Black Pepper
- 1/2 cup All-Purpose Flour
- 1/2 cup Bread Crumbs
- 1 large Egg
- 3 tablespoons Oil (for frying)
- German Cucumber Salad
- 4 small or 2 large Seedless Cucumber
- 1/2 cup Sour Cream
- 1 tablespoon White Vinegar
- 1 tablespoon chopped Dill

Direction

- Start by making the salad. Cut the cucumbers into thin rounds and chop the dill as finely as you can manage. In a bowl, add the sour cream, vinegar, salt and pepper and stir to combine. Now, add the cucumber slices, dill and mix. Cover and put it into the refrigerator while you make the Schnitzel.
- Next, tenderize and flatten the chicken breasts. The secret in making juicy Schnitzel is pounding the meat! Yes, we have to get these breasts nice and thin. This will ensure that the curst is nicely fired and crispy while the inside of the meat is fully cooked through and stays juicy. If your meat is too thick, the outside will be browned and ready but the inside of the meat will not have had enough time to properly cook through. On a large cutting board or a clean surface, place a large piece of cling film down, add your chicken breast, then cover it with another large piece of cling film (you can also use a zip-lock bag). I suggest doing one breast at a time if you are new to the meat pounding game. With a meat tenderizer/pounder/meat mallet (oh gosh so many names!!) OR what I like to use – a rolling pin, pound the chicken until it is about 1/3 – 1/2 inch thick. Next, season the chicken breast with salt & pepper on both sides and set them aside on a plate.
- Set up your breading station with one bowl and two-three plates. Crack an egg into the bowl and whisk. Add the flour to a plate and the breadcrumbs (I use Italian seasoned breadcrumbs) to another. I used my large, glass casserole dish. First, season the chicken breasts with salt & pepper on both sides. Next, dredge the chicken breast into the flour. Coat both sides well and shake off the excess. Next,

dip it into the egg and coat both sides. Lastly, dip it into the breadcrumbs! Make sure the chicken is well coated in the breadcrumb, because that is the best part!

- Let's head over to the stove. Heat up a large skillet with 3 tablespoons of oil. Olive, canola, or avocado oils are great. Once hot, carefully add the dredged chicken breasts to the hot oil. Cook them on medium-high heat for 3-4 minutes on each side. The internal temperature of the chicken should be at least 165°F.
- Time to plate up! It's very traditional to serve a slice or two of lemon with your Schnitzel, the juice of the lemon compliments the meat so well! Guten Appetit!

107. Seafood, Fennel And Lime Salad

Serving: Serves 4 | Prep: | Cook: |Ready in:

Ingredients

- 2 small fennel bulbs
- 1/2 red onion, very thinly sliced
- grated zest and juice of 1 lime
- 2 cloves garlic, crushed
- 2 tablespoons chopped dill
- 2 tablespoons chopped flat-leaf parsley
- 1 mild chile, seeded and finely chopped
- 4 tablespoons olive oil
- 8 tiger prawns
- 12 ounces 350g cleaned baby squid
- 1 tablespoon sumac
- 2 tablespoons chopped cilantro
- coarse sea salt
- pomegranate seeds for garnish (optional)

Direction

- 1. Trim the bases and tops of the fennel bulbs, then slice crosswise as thinly as you can. A mandoline would be useful here. In a large bowl, mix the fennel and red onion with the lime zest and juice, garlic, dill, parsley, chile, 2 tablespoons of the olive oil, and 1/2 teaspoon salt. Set aside.
- 2. To prepare the prawns, peel the shells away from the bodies, keeping the tail segment of the shell on. Cut a shallow slit along the back of each prawn and use the tip of a small knife to remove the dark vein.
- 3. Place a heavy cast-iron pan, preferably a ridged grill pan, over high heat and leave for a few minutes until piping hot. Meanwhile, mix the prawns and squid with the remaining 2 tablespoons oil and a pinch of salt. Grill them in small batches, turning them over after 1 minute and continuing until just done (about 1 more minute for the squid and 2 to 3 for the prawns). Transfer to a cutting board and slice the squid into thick rings. You can leave the prawns whole or cut them in half.
- 4. Add the seafood to the salad bowl and toss together. You can serve the salad immediately or leave it in the fridge for up to 1 day. To serve, stir in the sumac and cilantro, then taste and adjust the seasoning. When pomegranate seeds are available, they make a beautiful garnish.

108. Seafood, Fennel, And Lime Salad

Serving: Serves 4 | Prep: | Cook: |Ready in:

Ingredients

- 2 small fennel bulbs
- 1/2 red onion, very thinly sliced
- Grated zest and juice of 1 lime
- 2 cloves garlic, crushed
- 2 tablespoons chopped dill
- 2 tablespoons chopped flat-leaf parsley
- 1 mild chile, seeded and finely chopped
- 4 tablespoons olive oil
- 8 tiger prawns
- 12 ounces cleaned baby squid

- 1 tablespoon sumac
- 2 tablespoons chopped cilantro
- Coarse sea salt
- Pomegranate seeds for garnish (optional)

Direction

- Trim the bases and tops of the fennel bulbs, then slice crosswise as thinly as you can. A mandoline would be useful here. In a large bowl, mix the fennel and red onion with the lime zest and juice, garlic, dill, parsley, chile, 2 tablespoons of the olive oil, and 1/2 teaspoon salt. Set aside.
- To prepare the prawns, peel the shells away from the bodies, keeping the tail segment of the shell on. Cut a swallow slit along the back of each prawn and use the tip of a small knife to remove the dark vein.
- Place a heavy cast-iron pan, preferably a ridged grill pan, over high heat and leave for a few minutes until piping hot. Meanwhile, mix the prawns and squid with the remaining 2 tablespoons oil and a pinch of salt. Grill them in small batches, turning them over after 1 minute and continuing until just done (about 1 more minute for the squid and 2 to 3 for the prawns). Transfer to a cutting board and slice the squid into thick rings. You can leave the prawns whole or cut them in half.
- Add the seafood to the salad bowl and toss together. You can serve the salad immediately or leave it in the fridge for up to 1 day. To serve, stir in the sumac and cilantro, then taste and adjust the seasoning. When pomegranate seeds are available, they make a beautiful garnish.

109. Seared Salmon With Herbal Lemon Emulsion

Serving: Serves 4 | Prep: | Cook: |Ready in:

Ingredients

- Pan Seared Salmon
- 2 Wild Caught Salmon steaks, thick cut
- 1 tablespoon Organic Coconut Oil
- 1 tablespoon Organic Butter
- 1.5 teaspoons Salt, to taste
- 1/2 teaspoon Pepper, fresh cracked
- 3 Thyme, Fresh sprigs
- 1 tablespoon Sugar
- Parsley-Lemon Emulsion
- 1/2 cup Greek Olive Oil
- 1 Lemon
- 1 cup Organic Parsley (fresh)
- 1/2 teaspoon Salt
- 2 tablespoons Organic Dill (fresh)

Direction

- Dry cure salmon with 1 tsp salt and sugar. Sprinkle generously and set aside - 30 minutes Rinse, then pat dry with tea towel.
- Start emulsion by rough chopping parsley. Squeeze lemon into a bowl, then slowly drizzle olive oil, whisking while the mixture turns an opaque golden color. Season with salt. Add parsley and dill, whisk with fork to saturate. Set aside.
- Pre-heat oven to 400°. Heat cast iron skillet to medium, melt butter and coconut oil. Sear salmon each side 7-8m until golden brown. Flip, baste the salmon with a spoon with the butter and coconut oil. Cook another 7-8m. Halfway through, throw in thyme sprigs and continue basting.
- Allow salmon to rest for 4-5m, plate and serve with emulsion piled high on top of salmon.

110. Smoked Salmon Couscous {with Feta And Dill}

Serving: Serves 4 as a side, more if using in mushroom caps as appetizer | Prep: | Cook: |Ready in:

Ingredients

- 4 ounces Wild Smoked Salmon

- 1 to 1 1/2 cups Whole Wheat Couscous
- 3 to 5 ounces Crumbled Feta Cheese
- Handful Chopped Fresh Dill (reserve some for garnish)
- a few tablespoons Chopped Fresh Chives (reserve some for garnish)
- Black Pepper to taste
- Garlic Salt to taste
- Olive Oil
- optional: Roasted Baby Portobello Mushroom Caps

Direction

- Cook couscous according to package directions -or- add 1 cup couscous to 1 1/2 cups boiling water. Take off heat and let couscous sit for about 5 minutes and fluff with a fork. This will yield about 2 cups of fluffy couscous. Set aside.
- Toss couscous in a bowl with some olive oil, garlic salt and pepper.
- Add smoked salmon, feta cheese, some dill and chives. Gently combine. Adjust seasonings to taste. Add more or less of any ingredient if you wish.
- Top each serving with additional feta, dill and chives for garnish. So simple, so good!
- Serving idea: Serve Smoked Salmon Couscous on roasted baby Portobello mushroom caps.
- To roast mushroom caps: Preheat broiler with oven rack 4" away from heat source. Gently wipe clean mushroom caps. Lightly spray both sides of mushrooms with olive oil, sprinkle on garlic salt and pepper. Place on a baking sheet. Broil for about 2 minutes gill side up. Flip and broil the mushroom tops another two minutes. Dump out any liquid from mushrooms.
- Scoop a small amount of couscous into each mushroom cap and garnish with feta, dill and chives.

111. Smoked Salmon Pate

Serving: Serves 8-10 | Prep: | Cook: | Ready in:

Ingredients

- 1/2 pound smoked salmon, skinned
- 1/2 pound cream cheese, softened
- 1/3 cup green onion, finely chopped
- 1/4 cup fresh dill, finely chopped
- 1/2 lemon, juiced
- 1 small red onion, finely chopped
- 1 bottle capers, drained
- 1 loaf party rye or pumpernickel

Direction

- Mix salmon, cream cheese, green onion, dill and lemon juice in the food processor until well mixed and finely chopped, but not smooth. Pack into a small cereal bowl and chill. Turn out onto a nice serving platter; ring pate with red onion, then capers. Garnish with parsley. Serve with rye or pumpernickel slices or crostini.

112. Smoked Salmon And Pearl Cous Cous Salad

Serving: Serves 4 | Prep: | Cook: | Ready in:

Ingredients

- 4 cups cooked pearl cous-cous
- 8 ounces smoked salmon, torn into smallish pieces
- 2 cups arugula
- 1/2 cup kalamata olives, halved
- 1/2 cup sliced red onion
- 1/4 cup crumbled feta cheese
- 1/4 cup olive oil
- 1/4 cup fresh lemon juice
- 2 tablespoons chopped fresh dill
- salt and pepper to taste

Direction

- In a large bowl, lightly mix couscous, salmon, arugula, olives, onion and feta.
- In a small bowl whisk oil, lemon juice and dill to make the dressing.
- Pour dressing over couscous and lightly mix.
- Add salt and pepper to taste.
- Chill in fridge for at least 30 minutes. Enjoy!

113. Smoked Trout Spread

Serving: Serves 5 | Prep: | Cook: | Ready in:

Ingredients

- 1 packet cream cheese
- 1 packet smoked trout
- 1 teaspoon dried dill
- 1 splash lemon juice
- 1 pinch pepper

Direction

- With a fork, mix all the ingredients together in a bowl. Do not over mix and leave some chunks. Garnish with more dill.

114. Smoked Trout, Beet & Apple Salad With Trout Grebenes

Serving: Serves 4 | Prep: | Cook: | Ready in:

Ingredients

- 2 Filet Smoked Trout
- 6 Small steamed beets, peeled
- 1 tart green Apple
- Juice & Zest of 1 lemon
- Dill fronds to garnish
- vegetable oil
- Dairy Free Horseradish Dressin
- Creamy Horseradish Vinaigrette (Dairy Free)
- .5 cup silken tofu
- 1 .5 tablespoons apple cider vinegar
- 1 clove garlic, minced
- 1 small shallot, minced
- 1 tablespoon prepared horseradish or 1Tbs grated fresh
- 2 tablespoon olive oil
- ½ cup chopped dill & chives

Direction

- Squeeze half a lemon over shallot and let sit
- Skin trout and break in to bite size pieces, reserve skin for garnish
- Dice beets into cubes
- Peel apple and dice into cubes (same size as beets)
- Toss apples & beets with 1 tablespoon of Horseradish dressing
- Arrange beet and apple cubes + shallots over top
- Lay trout bits on top of that
- Scatter crisped trout skin & dill fronds over top
- Creamy Horseradish Vinaigrette (Dairy Free)
- Place tofu, vinegar, horseradish, garlic, shallots and ½ herbs in food processor
- Blend until pureed
- While processor is running, add water, followed by oil
- Season to taste with salt & pepper
- Stir in remaining herbs

115. Smoked Salmon Pasta

Serving: Serves 4 | Prep: | Cook: | Ready in:

Ingredients

- 1 leek (white and green)
- 2 tablespoons olive oil
- 2 tablespoons butter
- 2 tablespoons sun dry tomatoes puree
- 2 tablespoons fresh dill

- 1 cup 35% cream
- 6 ounces smoked salmon pieces
- salt and pepper
- 8 ounces fresh whole wheat pasta

Direction

- Clean, dice and wash leek.
- Sate with oil and butter for 5-6 minutes.
- Add sun dry tomatoes puree, cream, dill, salt and pepper. Let cook for 5 more minutes.
- Mix smoked salmon in and take off the stove.
- Mix with cooked pasta and serve with more dill.
- The sauce can be made ahead and mix whit pasta just before serving.

116. Spanakopita Frittata

Serving: Serves 8 | Prep: | Cook: | Ready in:

Ingredients

- 9 ounces Fresh Spinach
- 2 tablespoons Olive Oil
- 1 Yellow Onion (Chopped)
- 3 Garlic Cloves (Chopped)
- 4 Eggs
- 1 teaspoon Baking Powder
- 6 ounces Reduced Fat Feta
- 1/4 cup Fresh Dill (Chopped)
- 1/4 cup Fresh Parsley (Chopped)
- Salt and Pepper to taste

Direction

- Preheat oven to 350 degrees. Then in a medium pot sauté 1 onion with 3 garlic cloves in olive oil until fragrant and lightly brown.
- Next, stir in 9 ounces of fresh spinach and cook until wilted.
- Remove from heat and mix in eggs, baking powder, Feta (reduced fat), parsley, and dill until well incorporated. Season with salt and pepper to taste.
- Transfer the spinach mixture into a PAM sprayed pie or dish and bake at 350 degrees for 30 minutes or until lightly browned.

117. Spanakopita Grilled Cheese

Serving: Makes 2 sandwiches | Prep: | Cook: | Ready in:

Ingredients

- 1 tablespoon softened butter
- 4 slices good-quality bread (I used a Sicilian loaf studded with sesame seeds)
- 1 clove garlic, sliced thin
- 2 tablespoons olive oil
- 1 shallot, sliced thinly
- one 10-ounce bag baby spinach, or 2 big handfuls
- pinch salt and freshly cracked pepper
- 1 teaspoon chopped dill
- 2 ounces feta, crumbled
- 4 thin slices provolone cheese

Direction

- Either plug in your panini press (I'm old school so I use my default early 2000s wedding gift "George Foreman grill") or heat a skillet over medium heat. Divide butter evenly between the four slices of bread, spread thinly on one side of each slice.
- In a medium skillet, heat olive oil over medium-high heat, add the garlic and shallot, and cook 4 minutes, or until the garlic is golden-brown. Add spinach and salt and pepper, and cook for few minutes, until the spinach is wilted and most of the moisture is cooked out. Add dill and feta, turn off heat, and mix.
- Assemble the sandwiches by placing two slices of bread butter side-down on your press or pan, add one slice of provolone to each, then divide the spinach mixture in half and place half on each slice. Top with the

remaining 2 slices of cheese and slices of bread, butter side-up.
- If using a panini press, put the lid down and cook for about 5 minutes, or until golden and bubbly. If using a pan, flip after about 5 minutes, then cook on the other side for 3 minutes. Eat with tomato soup, if you so please.

118. Spinach Crepes With Smoked Salmon And Lemony Greek Yogurt Sauce

Serving: Serves 6 | Prep: | Cook: | Ready in:

Ingredients

- Crepes
- 1 package frozen chopped spinach, thawed, & squeezed in paper towels to remove excess moisture
- 3 large eggs (** or 2 large eggs & 2 egg whites)
- 1 1/2 cups Almond Milk
- 1/2 cup Brown Rice Flour
- 1/2 cup Quinoa Flour
- 1 bunch scallions, trimmed and minced (** white parts only)
- 1/3 cup fresh dill, chopped (** use fresh here .. it really does make a difference)
- Pinch of cayenne pepper
- salt & pepper, to taste
- 1/2 cup water + more if needed for thinning the batter
- 1-2 tablespoons coconut oil
- Filling
- 1 cup greek yogurt, plain
- 1 tablespoon grated lemon rind
- 1 tablespoon fresh lemon juice
- 2 shallots, finely minced
- 2 tablespoons capers, drained
- 2 teaspoons paprika
- 12 ounces peppered smoked salmon (** or smoked salmon sliced thin)

Direction

- To Make The Crepes
- Prepare the spinach by de-frosting & squeezing in paper towels to remove all of the excess moisture. Set aside.
- Blend the eggs and almond milk in a blender or food processor until well blended. Add the flours & blend until smooth.
- Add the spinach, scallions, half the dill, cayenne pepper, salt and pepper and blend again until very smooth. Stir in the water and allow the batter to rest for 15 minutes.
- Heat a seven- to eight-inch crepe pan over medium-high heat. Brush with coconut oil. Pour 1/3 cup of the batter into the pan, tilting it as you go, allowing the batter to evenly coat the bottom. Cook about two minutes, until lightly browned, turn the crepe over and cook about 30 seconds longer. Remove the crepe from the pan and repeat with the remaining batter, making 10 to 12 crepes
- To Make the Filling
- Combine the Greek yogurt, lemon peel, juice, shallots, remaining dill, capers and paprika. Spread each crepe with some of this mixture, then cover with a layer of smoked salmon.
- Roll the crepe & enjoy

119. Spinach Pie (spanakopita)

Serving: Makes 25 pieces | Prep: | Cook: | Ready in:

Ingredients

- for filling
- 3 pounds fresh spinach (we can also use 3 &1/2 pounds frozen spinach)
- 2 leeks chopped
- 1 medium onion chopped
- 1 bunch scallions chopped
- 1 bunch dill chopped
- 1/2 pound crumbled feta cheese
- 2 eggs

- 1/2 cup olive oil
- nutmeg, salt, black pepper
- 6 - 9 thick phyllo dough sheets (should be about 2 inches bigger, around your baking pan).
- plus olive oil for brushing
- for dough (in case you want to make your own phyllo dough)
- 2 pounds plus 2 cups all purpose flour
- 2 - 2,5 cups warm water
- 1/3 cup olive oil
- 1 tablespoon vinegar
- 1,5 teaspoons salt

Direction

- INSTRUCTIONS for phyllo dough
- In a big bowl put the half flour, salt, olive oil, vinegar and the half of warm water. Stir until forms soft dough, then knead and add little by little the remaining flour and water. The dough should be silky, pliant, and smooth. Cover and let it rest at room temperature at least 30 minutes before using. Divide the dough into 9 or 6 equal parts. Using a rolling pin make the phyllo sheets and use each one immediately.
- INSTRUCTIONS for filling
- Clean vegetables very well. Chop them.
- Grab a small amount of spinach put it in a strainer and rub the leaves to wilt. Continue until you finish the spinach. Press firmly spinach to drain any remaining liquids and let it sit for 30 minutes in the strainer.
- However, for our convenience: Steam the spinach, put it in a strainer press it and let it drain very well.
- In a shallow wide saucepan sauté chopped onion, leeks and scallions with 1/2 cup olive oil over medium/ high heat.
- Add spinach and continue sauté. Reduce heat to low/medium and cook for 15 minutes.
- Add chopped dill, salt (watch out, because we've already seasoned the spinach, may not needed more salt), pepper and nutmeg and cook for additional 5 minutes.

- Remove from heat and let it cool. Add eggs and stir. Add crumbled feta cheese and stir again.
- Preheat the oven to 350° F.
- Oil a baking pan and lay 3 phyllo sheets brushing with olive oil (about a tablespoon) each one.
- Spread the half of filling.
- Lay other 3 phyllo sheets brushing them too.
- Spread the remaining filling.
- Lay the last 3 phyllo sheets always brushing each one with olive oil *.
- Cut the pie into pieces. Bake for about an hour until it becomes golden.
- * We also can use 2+2+2 phyllo sheets or 3 sheets to the bottom and 3 on top.

120. Spring's Beauty In A Bowl: A Simple Six Piece Salad

Serving: Serves 4 | Prep: | Cook: |Ready in:

Ingredients

- Salad
- 1 hefty handfuls Arugula
- 2 handfuls Microgreens (kale, cilantro, radish sprouts)
- 1 handful Fresh Garden Peas
- 1 handful Cherry Tomatoes
- 1-2 bulbs Spring Onion
- 1-2 handfuls Sunflower Sees
- Creamy Curried Lemony Dill Dressing
- 1/2 a block Tofu
- 1 clove Garlic
- 1 Lemon, juiced
- 1/2 - 1 teaspoons Dill
- 1/4 teaspoon Curry Powder (more if you like spice)
- 1 teaspoon Olive Oil
- Fresh Cracked Black Pepper (to taste)

Direction

- Rinse and pat dry your greens. Add to a salad bowl. Pinch your pea pods to open them, then loosen each pea with your finger to release them into your salad bowl. Slice the cherry tomatoes in half, and the spring onion into thin rounds. Add the tomatoes and onions to your salad. Put the tofu and garlic into a small electric blender and blend until the tofu is creamy and the garlic is completely mashed. Cut your lemon in half and squeeze in the juice. Add the dill and curry powder and mix well. Drizzle in the olive oil and just lightly pulse a few times. Crack the pepper in and just light stir with a spatula. Taste and adjust lemon, spices, and add, maybe, a pinch of salt. Use the spatula to pour the dressing over the salad. The consistency will be thick, but once tossed, the greens, tomatoes, and peas will add their moisture to give it a beautiful balance between creamy and crunchy, soft and snappy, soothing and fresh. Garnish with a generous helping of sunflower seeds, and a sprig of fresh rosemary. I also tossed into the salad a handful of fresh cilantro. I love treating mint, cilantro, and parsley as if they are more than garnish, but leaves with their own rightful place in the salad.

- Cook squash and onion in broth over medium high heat until tender-about 15 minutes.
- Puree the contents of squash, onions and broth in blender. Do in small batches, as to not burn yourself with the hot liquid.
- Return the pureed mixture to the pot and add the half and half. Cook on medium low for 3-4 minutes.
- Remove one cup of the mixture and pour in a separate bowl. Slowly whisk in the sour cream to the separate bowl, as to not curdle the soup. Return the soup/sour cream mixture to the pot.
- Season with salt and freshly ground pepper. Distribute between bowls and sprinkle with fresh dill. Serve immediately.

121. Squash Soup

Serving: Serves 4 | Prep: | Cook: |Ready in:

Ingredients

- 6 medium squash, cut into one-inch chunks
- 1 medium onion, chopped coursely
- 2 cups chicken broth
- 1 cup half and half
- 1/2 cup sour cream
- salt and pepper to tase
- fresh dill

Direction

122. Sticky, Spicy, Sweet Roasted Carrots And Chickpeas With Date Vinaigrette

Serving: Serves 4 | Prep: | Cook: |Ready in:

Ingredients

- 1 1/2 pounds carrots, peeled and halved (or quartered, depending on size) into thin, uniform slices
- 1 15-ounce can of chickpeas, drained and rinsed
- 1 teaspoon Aleppo pepper
- 1 teaspoon cumin seed, lightly crushed
- 1 teaspoon coriander seed, lightly crushed
- kosher salt, to taste
- a few tablespoons of coarsely chopped dill or cilantro
- For Date Vinaigrette:
- 5 Medjool dates, pitted and chopped into small pieces
- 1 small garlic clove, roughly chopped
- 1/4 cup cup sherry vinegar, plus additional to taste
- Finely grated lemon zest plus 2 tablespoons lemon juice, from 1 small lemon

- kosher salt, to taste
- 1/3 cup extra-virgin olive oil
- 2 to 4 tablespoons warm water

Direction

- To make the date vinaigrette, combine the dates, garlic, sherry vinegar, lemon zest, lemon juice, and a pinch of kosher salt, stirring a few times to ensure the dates and garlic are fully submerged. Do this step in the blender jar if using a stand blender, or a glass measuring cup or other suitable container if using a stick blender. Let macerate for 20 to 30 minutes while prepping the carrots and other ingredients.
- Heat oven to 400 degrees F.
- Add the extra-virgin olive oil and the warm water (starting with 2 tablespoons) to the macerated dates and garlic in the blender jar. Blend until the vinaigrette is smooth, adding a few more teaspoons of warm water at a time to thin the vinaigrette. You're looking for a slightly thick vinaigrette, but one that can still be drizzled or poured. Add salt and sherry vinegar, to taste.
- Place the carrots and chickpeas on a sheet pan or baking dish lined with parchment that's large enough to fit them in a single, even layer. Toss with 1/4 cup of the date vinaigrette, Aleppo pepper, cumin seed, coriander seed, and a few large pinches of kosher salt until evenly coated. It may seem like too much vinaigrette, but it'll reduce down and coat the carrots and chickpeas—so don't skimp! Spread the carrots and chickpeas in a single, even layer. Roast until the carrots and chickpeas are golden and the carrots are fork-tender, stirring 4 to 5 times to ensure even roasting and to avoid the vinaigrette burning in open areas of the pan (but don't be too concerned--it's why you're using parchment!). The roasting time will depend on the freshness and size of the carrots – anywhere from 25 minutes to 45+ minutes. If the carrots are browning too quickly but aren't tender, lower the oven to 375 degrees F and continue roasting until tender.
- Scatter the dill or cilantro over the carrots and chickpeas, and adjust seasoning to taste. Serve warm, making sure to drizzle more of the vinaigrette over the carrots and chickpeas before serving. (See headnote for suggested pairings.)

123.   Stovetop Smoked Sturgeon A La Russe

Serving: Serves 2 | Prep: | Cook: | Ready in:

Ingredients

- A cheap roasting pan, rack, and aluminum foil
- A handful of alder chips for smoking
- 1 Sturgeon steak about a pound
- 1 Slice of bacon cut into batons
- 1 Clove of garlic minced
- 1/4 Medium onion sliced fine
- 1 or 2 Celery stalks cut into 2 inch batons
- 1/4 to 1/3 English cucumber peeled and cut into thick batons
- 2 or 3 Small kosher dill pickles cut into thick matchsticks
- 2 ounces Cream
- Chopped fresh dill for garnish

Direction

- Most likely you'll have a sturgeon steak that's a bit less than a pound. I cut the two filets off the backbone for two servings although you could leave it whole until after it's cooked. Put alder chips (one nice handful) in the center of the roasting pan, place the rack on top of the pan and the fish (cleaned and dry) on top of the rack then make a tent of foil and crimp it well all around the edges of the pan. It will take about a half hour to smoke so plan accordingly.
- Place your smoker over a burner and turn on high. In four or five minutes you should see

- smoke escaping. Turn the burner off, leave the fish covered and wait 30 minutes. At the end of 30 minutes, the fish should be perfectly cooked. If it's a bit under done give it another blast of heat for a minute or two. If it's overdone curse me all you want.
- While the fish is smoking, lightly sauté one slice of bacon cut into lardoons with about a quarter of thinly sliced onion and a clove of garlic cut into julienne. Cut one or two celery stalks into thin batons one to two inches long and blanch for two or three minutes. Peel and cut the cucumber the same length, remove the seeds and cut into small wedges say a quarter inch thick. Blanch for a couple of minutes. For pickles I used 3 Zergüt kosher dill pickles cut into batons about an eighth of an inch. They're small, no more than a couple of inches long. What I aimed for was more or less equal amounts of onion, celery, cucumber, and pickle but this time you're going to eat this not me. Do what you like. Toss the celery, cucumber pickle in with the bacon and onion, wet it with a little cream (it's your waist and your taste) and cook it enough so it's not too runny. The vegetables are now ready.
- Plate the vegetables, put the fish on top, and garnish with chopped fresh dill if you have it. Don't be shy and eat the yellow fat, it really picks up the smoke. BTW it's unlikely that you'll ever use that pan for anything but a smoker after this. It warps and gets wicked stains but clean it up for lots of other smoked fish possibilities. Clean up isn't so bad when the kitchen smells of alder and smoked fish.

124. Stuffed Bell Peppers

Serving: Serves 6 (2 per portion) or 12 if serving with a side dish | Prep: | Cook: | Ready in:

Ingredients

- For the Tomato Sauce (makes 4 1/2 to 5 cups)
- • 1/4 cup olive oil, I used Kalamata olive oil
- • 1 large Spanish or yellow onion, diced
- • 4 garlic cloves, peeled and thinly sliced
- • 1 1/2 teaspoons kosher salt
- • 1 medium carrot, shredded
- • 1 medium parsley root or parsnip, shredded
- • 2 celery ribs, diced
- • 1/2 teaspoon red pepper flakes
- • 2 (28-ounce) cans crushed tomatoes and their juice
- • 1/4 cup red wine vinegar + 2 tablespoons packed light brown sugar
- • 3 tablespoons of each, chopped fresh mint leaves and dill or parsley and dill
- For the filling
- • 1 pound beef chuck, ground
- • 1 pound lamb shoulder, ground
- • 1/2 cup uncooked white long grain rice
- • 1 medium roughly chopped Spanish or yellow onion
- • 1 teaspoon kosher salt
- • 1/2 teaspoon freshly ground black pepper
- • 2 tablespoons fresh mint leaves, chopped
- • 6 large red or any color you like bell peppers, washed, cut in half lengthwise, seeds and membranes removed

Direction

- For the Tomato Sauce (makes 4 1/2 to 5 cups)
- To make the sauce: heat the olive oil in a large saucepan, add the onions and garlic, salt and red pepper flakes; cook over medium-low heat for 8 to 10 minutes, until translucent. Add carrot, parsley root or parsnip and celery; cook for a few more minutes, until they are quite soft.
- Add tomatoes, vinegar and brown sugar. Bring to a boil, stirring often; then lower the heat and simmer uncovered for 30 minutes, stirring occasionally. Of the heat mix-in mint and dill. Set aside. This sauce holds 1 week in the refrigerator or up to 2 months in the freezer.
- For the filling
- Preheat the oven to 350 degrees F.
- To prepare the filling: Place rice in a small bowl and cover with boiling water; cool to

room temperature and then drain well but do not wash. Cut the meat in 1-inch cubes and run it through a meat grinder together with the chopped onion to a large bowl. Combine the ground meat and onion mixture, the drained rice, salt, black pepper, mint and 1 heaping cup of the tomato sauce; mix well.

- To assemble: In the bottom of a 12-inch in diameter/2 1/2-inches deep cast iron skillet or a large casserole dish, place a few celery ribs so they cover the bottom of the dish. This step will prevent the peppers from sticking or burning. Then spread about 1 1/2 cups of the tomato sauce; fill the bell pepper halves with about 1/2 cup of the filling and lay them out in one layer on top. Evenly cover with the remaining sauce. Cover the dish tightly with a lid or with parchment and foil; place on a rimmed baking sheet and transfer to the oven.
- Bake for 1 hour or until the meat is cooked and the rice is tender. Serve hot, topped with as much sauce as you like. It is also very tasty to crumble some good feta over the top or like most people in Eastern Europe, with a dollop of sour cream or a Greek yogurt with mint, lemon zest, salt and freshly ground black pepper sauce.

125. Stuffed Grape Leaves & Tzatziki Sauce

Serving: Serves 10 | Prep: 0hours20mins | Cook: 1hours0mins | Ready in:

Ingredients

- Grape Leaves
- 1 pound Ground beef
- 1 cup Uncooked jasmine rice
- 3 Garlic cloves, minced
- 1 teaspoon Salt
- 1/2 teaspoon Pepper
- 1 teaspoon Cloves
- 1 teaspoon Allspice
- 16 ounces Jar of grape leaves
- 1/3 cup Olive oil
- 1/3 cup Lemon juice
- 1/3 cup Chicken broth
- Tzatziki Sauce
- 3 Garlic cloves
- 1/2 Large cucumber, peeled and chopped in large pieces
- 1 Bunch fresh dill leaves
- 1 Lemon, juiced
- 1 teaspoon Salt
- 1 tablespoon Sugar
- 2 tablespoons Soy sauce
- 1/2 teaspoon cumin
- 2 cups sour cream

Direction

- Grape Leaves
- Place 1 cup of the rice and 2 cups of water in a small saucepan, and bring to a boil.
- Reduce heat to low and cook until all the liquid is absorbed, about 15 minutes.
- Place cooked rice in a large mixing bowl, add beef and spices, and mix well.
- Carefully pull the leaves out of the jar and strain off the liquid.
- To roll the leaves, place one in front of you and put a spoonful of the filling in the center of the leave. Put more filling in the bigger leaves, and less in the smaller leaves.
- Roll the bottom of the leave over the filling tightly, then roll each side over to the center, and then roll up until sealed.
- Place the leaves seam side down in a large baking pan.
- Whisk olive oil, lemon juice, and chicken broth together until thickened; pour over the grape leaves.
- Cover with foil and bake at 350* for 1 hour.
- Tzatziki Sauce
- Place garlic, cucumber, and dill in food processor, turn to high until finely chopped.
- Transfer to a medium sized bowl and add the other ingredients.
- Mix well and serve with the grape leaves.

126. Stuffed Mussels Mussels Dolmas

Serving: Makes 14 mussel dolmas | Prep: | Cook: | Ready in:

Ingredients

- Stuffing
- 14 teaspoons White jasmine rice (1 tsp for each mussel)
- 1/2 cup Onion, chopped
- 2 tablespoons Olive oil
- 1 teaspoon Salt
- 1 teaspoon Black pepper, ground
- 1/2 cup Parsley, chopped
- 1/2 cup Dill, chopped
- 1 tablespoon Mint, dried
- 3 cups Water, boiling (divided)
- 1 Lemon (juice)
- 1 teaspoon Clove powder (optional-highly recommended)
- Mussels
- 14 Mussels
- 1 cup Water

Direction

- Put your mussels into salted water at least one hour ago. After that time discard any open or broken shelled mussels. Debeard and clean each of them thoroughly with a brush, use a knife to scratch if needed.
- In a medium pot add the olive oil and onion and cook until the onions are tender but not brown.
- Wash rice and add to the pot. Stir occasionally until the water of rice evaporates.
- After rice gets sticky to each other add boiling water and simmer.
- Add salt and black pepper. Cover the pot until almost evaporates.
- When you see the holes in rice turn off the heat and add dried mint, dill and parsley and stir.
- In a large pot bring the water boil.
- Add mussels and cover the pot. Cook until all the mussels are open, 3-5 minutes.
- Rinse mussels with cold water. Working one at a time, set apart the shells. Pull apart the flesh. Put 2 teaspoons of stuffing (or as needed) into one of the shells and top with the flesh and cover it with the other shell.
- Repeat this for every mussel and serve it with lemon pieces.

127. Summer Harvest Soup With Chilled Dill Yogurt

Serving: Serves 6-8 | Prep: | Cook: | Ready in:

Ingredients

- Summer Harvest Soup
- 2 medium yellow onions, sliced
- 1 small head of garlic, pressed
- 1/4 cup olive oil
- 1 1/2 teaspoons fresh celery blossoms (or 1/2 teaspoon dried celery seeds)
- pinch sea salt
- pinch cayenne pepper
- 1/2 cup dry white wine
- 3 cups small butterball potatoes, diced
- 4-5 cups chicken stock (homemade if possible)
- 6 cups mixed summer squash, diced
- pinch ground white pepper
- 1/8 cup fresh dill fronds, coarsely chopped
- Chilled Dill Yogurt
- 6 ounces plain yogurt (creamy greek yogurt or sheep yogurt if you can find it)
- 2 cloves garlic, pressed
- 1/2 Meyer Lemon, juice
- 1/2 Meyer Lemon, zest
- 1 teaspoon fresh dill, chopped
- tiny pinch sea salt

Direction

- In a large stock pot or Dutch oven, heat olive oil over low heat. Add onions, garlic, celery blossoms, cayenne, and pinch of salt. Stew covered over low heat for about 15 minutes until onions have softened.
- When onions are soft, turn up heat on stove to medium and lightly caramelize the onions.
- Pour white wine into the pot and scrape any browned tasty onion bits from the bottom. Cook to reduce wine by half.
- Add diced butterball potatoes and chicken stock. Simmer until potatoes are tender.
- Add squash (and a cup of water or stock if the liquid looks too low). Cover pot and continue to simmer until everything is tender.
- Let cool to room temp and then coarsely blend with an immersion blender. Adjust seasoning by adding salt if necessary. Toss in the chopped dill fronds and sprinkle a bit of ground white pepper.
- Reheat soup to serve warm. In the meantime, combine all ingredients for the Chilled Dill Yogurt.
- Garnish soup with a dollop of the Chilled Dill Yogurt and maybe even an extra sprig of dill.
- Enjoy!

128. Superiority Burger's BBQ Baked Gigante Beans With Polenta & Coleslaw

Serving: Serves 8 (and makes 2 cups chickpea mayo, 12 polenta planks) | Prep: 14hours0mins | Cook: 4hours0mins | Ready in:

Ingredients

- Baked beans and assembly
- 1 pound dried gigante beans, soaked overnight
- Grapeseed oil
- 1 medium yellow onion, finely chopped
- 4 garlic cloves, minced
- 8 cups water
- 2 tablespoons espresso (Superiority Burger uses Café Bustelo)
- 1/2 cup pureed tomatoes
- 1/4 cup firmly packed dark brown sugar
- 4 teaspoons Gulden's brown mustard
- 2 tablespoons molasses
- 2 tablespoons Frank's RedHot sauce
- 1/4 cup extra virgin olive oil
- 2 cups shredded green cabbage
- 2 tablespoons chopped fresh dill
- 1/2 cup Chickpea Mayo (see below)
- Juice of 1 lemon
- 8 Polenta Planks (see below)
- Chickpea mayo and polenta planks
- 1/2 cup liquid from a chickpea can
- 20 individual chickpeas
- 1 1/2 tablespoons Dijon mustard
- 2 tablespoons cider vinegar
- 1 tablespoon cane sugar
- 2 teaspoons kosher salt, plus more to taste
- 2 1/2 cups grapeseed oil
- Extra virgin olive oil
- 7 cups water
- 2 cups high-quality polenta (Superiority Burger uses Anson Mills)

Direction

- Baked beans and assembly
- Preheat the oven to 300° F.
- Drain the beans and put in a sturdy oven-safe pot, like a Dutch oven. In a medium pot over medium-high heat, add enough grape seed oil to coat the bottom. Add the onion and cook until soft and translucent, about 12 minutes. Add the garlic and cook until not raw anymore, basically. Add the water, espresso powder, tomato puree, brown sugar, mustard, molasses, and hot sauce and bring to a rolling boil. Remove the pot from the heat and pour the liquid over the beans. Add the olive oil to the beans and juice.
- Cover tightly with aluminum foil or a lid and put in the oven. This is going to take a while. Check after 2 hours and make sure not too much of the liquid has evaporated. If it has, just add more water, cover, and cook some

more. Check every hour or so until the beans are tender. Remove from the oven and season generously with salt and pepper. Let sit — the beans will absorb a lot of this liquid and release starch to make a thick sauce.
- Mix together the cabbage with the dill, mayo, lemon juice, and some salt and pepper in a medium bowl. In a large nonstick or cast-iron skillet set over medium heat, heat a few tablespoons of grape seed oil until shimmering. For each serving, sear a polenta plank on one side until golden brown and a little crispy, then flip it and sear the other side. Transfer to a plate, top generously with beans and bean sauce, and finish with a mound of the cabbage slaw.
- Chickpea mayo and polenta planks
- Make the chickpea mayo. Combine the chickpea liquid, chickpeas, mustard, cider vinegar, sugar, and salt in a tall container just large enough to fit the head of an immersion blender. Blend at high speed until the mixture is completely smooth and all the whole chickpeas are broken down. While the blender is running, slowly drizzle in the grape seed oil. As you add the oil, an emulsion will form and it will begin to thicken. Check the seasoning for salt and sugar. This will keep, covered, in the refrigerator for about 1 week.
- Make the polenta planks. Lightly grease a quarter sheet pan or an 8-inch square baking pan with a little bit of olive oil. Bring the water to a boil in a medium saucepan over high heat. Add salt and taste the water — it should taste well-seasoned. While whisking, pour the polenta into the boiling water. Simmer for 15 to 20 minutes, whisking occasionally. When ready, check the seasoning again for salt and then carefully pour the hot polenta into the pan and smooth the top as evenly as possible. Let set up at room temperature for at least 30 minutes. It will cut most easily into clean pieces if refrigerated for a couple hours or overnight. Cut into 12 planks.

129. Sweet And Spicy Quick Pickled Veggies

Serving: Makes 2 quarts | Prep: | Cook: |Ready in:

Ingredients

- Jar sized vegetables — I used a mix of green beans, carrots, and Persian cucumber, but the sky's the limit!
- 3 tablespoons kosher salt
- 2 tablespoons sugar
- 1 1/4 cups distilled white vinegar
- 2 tablespoons coriander seeds
- 1 tablespoon peppercorns
- 6 large garlic cloves, halved
- 4-6 dried hot chiles, I used Arbol
- 10 sprigs of dill

Direction

- Pack vegetables into 2 clean 1-quart glass jars. In a bowl, combine the salt, sugar, vinegar, coriander, peppercorns, and garlic. Whisk until the salt and sugar dissolve. Add 2 cups o water and pour the brine over the vegetables. Tuck the chiles and dill between the vegetables. Tightly close the jars and refrigerate overnight or for up to 1 month. Alternatively, you could follow proper canning procedures to preserve them.

130. Tangy Creamy Buttermilk Cucumbers

Serving: Serves 6 | Prep: | Cook: |Ready in:

Ingredients

- 3 cucumbers-sliced thinly
- 1 onion-sliced into thin rounds
- 1 cup buttermilk
- 1 cup sour cream
- 3 tablespoons apple cider vinegar
- 3 tablespoons sugar

- 1 teaspoon dried dill
- 2 tablespoons fresh dill
- 1/4 teaspoon salt and pepper
- 1 teaspoon minced garlic
- 1 teaspoon paprika

Direction

- Combine the cucumbers and onions in a deep bowl
- In a separate bowl, whisk together the buttermilk, sour cream, vinegar, sugar, dill, salt, pepper, garlic and paprika.
- Pour the buttermilk over the vegetables and refrigerate for an hour.

131. The American Black Forest

Serving: Serves 2 | Prep: | Cook: | Ready in:

Ingredients

- 1/2 pound premium, authentic smoked if possible, Black Forest ham, sliced thinly
- unsalted premium butter for bread slices
- 1/4 cup finely grated raw red cabbage
- 1/4 cup grated fresh cooked beet
- 1/4 cup grated crisp apple, jonagold or honey crisp
- 1 tablespoon finely minced red onion
- 10 gherkins, julienned
- 1 tablespoon finely grated celeriac
- 1 tablespoon finely grated fresh fennel
- 2 tablespoons chopped premium dried cranberries
- pink himalayan salt to taste
- 1 teaspoon fresh lemon juice
- cooked beet greens, chopped, optional
- 2 teaspoons champagne or pear vinegar
- 3 tablespoons sour cream
- 3 tablespoons mayonnaise
- 1 tablespoon Russian mustard
- 1 tablespoon chopped fresh dill
- 4 slices of multigrain artisan bread, the kind you love
- 8-10 gherkins for side garnish

Direction

- Toss the grated cabbage, beet, apple, onion, celeriac, fennel, cranberries, lemon juice and vinegar together with salt to taste. Let this sit for at least half an hour.
- Combine the sour cream, mayonnaise, dill, and mustard together.
- Evenly spread a thin layer of butter on each slice of bread for flavor and to keep the bread from getting soggy.
- Add the sliced ham on top of the bottom slice for each sandwich. Spread the sour cream/mayo dressing generously on top of the ham.
- Strain the cabbage topping from any liquid and spoon on top of the sour cream dressing. Add optional cooked chopped greens if desired. Add more sour cream/mayo dressing if desired on top of the cabbage mix and julienned gherkins. Add the top slice of buttered bread. Serve with gherkins.

132. Toasted Farro Salad With Roasted Leeks And Root Vegetables

Serving: Serves 4 | Prep: | Cook: | Ready in:

Ingredients

- 2 leeks
- 2 medium turnips, trimmed, peeled, and sliced into 1/2 inch-thick half moons
- 1 large rutabaga, trimmed, peeled, and sliced into 1/2 inch-thick half moons
- 1/4 cup extra-virgin olive oil, divided
- Sea salt, to taste
- Ground black pepper, to taste
- 3/4 cup dry farro
- Zest of 1 lemon plus 2 tablespoons juice

- 1/4 cup minced parsley, divided
- 2 tablespoons minced dill, divided
- 1/4 cup crumbled farmer's cheese

Direction

- Preheat the oven to 400° F. Move oven shelf to the top third of the oven. For easy cleanup, line one large and one small baking sheet with parchment.
- Trim the dark green section from the leeks, and halve lengthwise. Immerse leeks in water and shake out any sand and excess water. Trim the roots, and cut each half into 3-inch segments. In a medium-sized bowl, toss the leeks with 2 tablespoons olive oil, sea salt, and pepper. Spread the leeks out on the small baking sheet.
- In the same bowl used for the leeks, toss the turnip and rutabaga half-moons with 1 tablespoon olive oil, sea salt, and black pepper. Spread out on the large baking sheet.
- Slide both baking sheets into the oven and roast for 20 minutes. Use a spatula to flip the turnips and rutabagas. The leeks should roast for 20 to 25 minutes, or until quite soft with browned edges. Roast the turnips and rutabagas until edges are nicely browned, 30 to 35 minutes total.
- Meanwhile, cook the farro. Set a large pot of salted water over high heat to boil. Set a large skillet over medium-high heat, add the dry farro, and, shaking the pan frequently, toast just until farro browns slightly and is fragrant, about 2 minutes. Add farro to the salted water and simmer for 20 minutes, or until farro still has a little bite. Drain, toss with 2 tablespoons lemon juice and 3 tablespoons minced parsley, and set aside.
- Toss the farmer's cheese with 2 tablespoons olive oil, lemon zest, sea salt, pepper, and a tablespoon each minced parsley and dill.
- To plate the salad, toss the farro with the roasted turnips and rutabagas. Top with roasted leeks, crumbled farmers cheese, and remaining dill and parsley, and toss gently.

133. Topinambour Soup With Black Trumpets

Serving: Serves 6 | Prep: | Cook: | Ready in:

Ingredients

- 700 g tapinambour
- 1 onion
- 1 carrot
- 200 ml cream
- 200 ml beef stock(or vegetable stock)
- black sesame seeds
- dill
- 2 tablespoons olive oil
- 300 g Black Trumpet Mushrooms
- 1 tablespoon butter
- salt&pepper

Direction

- Peel the earth apples. Cut the carrots and the earth apples in cubes. Add olive oil in a pan, sweat your diced onions. Add the carrots cook for 1-2 minutes and then add the earth apples.
- Add the stock and simmer for 15-20 minute until they are soft. Blend them in a blender.
- Sauté the mushrooms.
- Put the puree back in the pan, adjust the seasoning. Pour the cream on top. Add the sautéed mushrooms and simmer.
- Sprinkle some chopped dill and roasted sesame seeds on top.

134. Traditional Sweet And Savory Finnish Christmas Pastries "Joulutortut"

Serving: Serves 4 | Prep: | Cook: | Ready in:

Ingredients

- For the savory pastries

- • 4 (5by 5-inches) Puff pastry squares
- • 3/4 cup whole milk ricotta, drained
- • 1/2 cup good quality feta (Greek or French)
- • 1large egg yolk
- • 2 teaspoons lemon zest
- • 2 teaspoons fresh dill, diced
- • 4 scallions, only the green part, chopped
- • 1/4 teaspoon freshly ground white or black pepper
- • 1 large egg yolk mixed with some water, for egg wash
- • Sesame seeds, toasted, for the top
- For the sweet pastries
- • 4 (5by 5-inches) Puff pastry squares
- • 1/2 cup Plum Jam
- • 1/3 cup fine ground walnuts
- • 2 teaspoons lemon or orange zest
- • 1 teaspoon pure vanilla extract
- • Pinch of coarse salt
- • Confectioners' sugar for dusting the tops

Direction

- To make filling for savory pastries: In a medium mixing bowl combine ricotta, feta, egg yolk, lemon zest, dill, scallions and pepper. Stir well until the mixture is homogeneous. Set aside.
- To make filling for sweet pastries: In a small mixing bowl combine Plum jam, walnuts, lemon or orange zest, vanilla and salt. Stir well until the mixture is homogeneous. Set aside.
- Preheat oven to 400 degrees F. Line two cookie baking sheets with parchment paper.
- Make cuts from the corners of each square about half way to the center; place a spoonful of savory filling in the center and fold every second section into the center, pinch tightly to form a windmill or a star shape, (which mine don't look like).
- Place on the baking sheet; brush with egg yolk; sprinkle with sesame seeds and transfer to the middle rack of the oven. Bake for 18-20 minutes until the pastries are puffed and golden.
- Repeat the same process with the sweet filling, only there is no need to brush them with the egg wash, since they will be dusted with confectioners' sugar.
- Serve warm or at room temperature for breakfast or brunch with a fragrant cup of tea or fresh espresso.

135. Tsukune "Matzah Ball" Soup

Serving: Serves 8 | Prep: 0hours30mins | Cook: 1hours0mins | Ready in:

Ingredients

- Tsukune (Chicken Meatball)
- 1 pound ground chicken
- 1 tablespoon cooking sake
- 1 egg, beaten
- 3 tablespoons matzah meal
- 1 leek, finely chopped and rinsed well
- 1 tablespoon peeled and grated ginger
- 1 teaspoon sea salt
- Soup Ingredients
- 3 carrots, peeled and cut at about 1" diagonals
- 2 turnips, peeled and cut into 1" cubes
- 1/4 cup fresh chopped dill
- chicken broth, about 62 ounces (store-bought works in a pinch, but homemade is many times better!)

Direction

- Place your chicken stock in a large pot and begin to heat it on the stove over medium heat. Sprinkle in salt until it's salted to your liking. Be careful not to over-salt- the meatballs have salt in them and remember you can always add more salt later.
- When the stock comes to a boil, lower the heat to low and add the carrots and turnips. Cover the pot and set a timer for 30 minutes (you can move on to making the tsukune at this point). If the timer has beeped for the carrots and turnips while you are in the middle of forming

the meatballs, check the carrots and turnips for done-ness. If they are perfectly cooked (still slightly firm but not mushy or crunchy), remove them from the broth with a slotted spoon and set aside. Keep the stock on low heat while you prepare the tsukune.
- Prep and combine the first seven ingredients for tsukune into a large mixing bowl and mix until everything is well-incorporated. Using two small spoons (about 2" x 1"), scoop the mixture onto one spoon, then use the other to start forming a sort of egg-shaped meatball. Spoon the mixture onto each spoon, going back and forth until it looks smooth, then drop it into the stock. Continue this until all meatballs are in the pot. They will be ready when they start floating to the top- about 5 minutes.
- When the meatballs are done, place the carrots and turnips back in, toss in the chopped dill, give it a good stir and serve immediately. I like to serve three meatballs per person.

136. Turkish Style Red Lentil Soup With Purple Carrots

Serving: Serves 4-6 | Prep: | Cook: |Ready in:

Ingredients

- 1 cup red lentils
- 600 milliliters vegetable broth(or water)
- 1 onion
- 1 purple potato
- 2 black carrots
- 6-8 sun-dried tomatoes (1 tbs tomato paste)
- 1 teaspoon coriander
- salt&pepper
- 1-2 dried chili pepper
- 2-3 tablespoons olive oil
- lemon wedge
- dill

Direction

- Dice the onions, carrots, potatoes and dried tomatoes. In a large pot add the olive oil, heat and add the onions, season and sweat at a medium low heat.
- Add the carrots and diced tomatoes and stir. Add the lentils. Top it with vegetable broth (or water). Combine everything and simmer until lentils are soft and fall apart. Add hot water if necessary.
- Remove the pot from the heat and use an immersion blender to blend the soup until it is creamy but not completely puréed. Or just leave it as it is for a more rustic look.
- Serve it with a lemon wedge and some chopped dill on top.

137. Twice Baked Smoked Salmon Mashed Potatoes

Serving: Serves 4-6 | Prep: | Cook: |Ready in:

Ingredients

- 4 large russet potatoes
- 225 grams hot smoked salmon
- 125 grams cream cheese
- 2 cups chopped fresh dill
- 2 green onions, thinly sliced
- 1 1/2 tablespoons grainy mustard
- 1 cup cream, heavy or light is up to you
- lots of sea salt and freshly cracked black pepper
- 2 cups shredded gruyere

Direction

- Bake the potatoes at 400 degrees F directly on the rack until tender all the way through, about 50~60 minutes.
- Cool slightly so they don't burn your hands, then halve them. Scoop out the flesh and mash it with salmon, cream cheese, dill, onions, and mustard. Season with salt and lots of pepper. The mixture will be dry and crumbly, so gradually stir in the cream until moist.

- Spread mixture into a baking dish and top with gruyere. I like to grate a bit of nutmeg to finish it off.
- Bake at 400 degrees F until heated through and the cheese is bubbly and golden, about 20 minutes.

138.   Vegan Mushroom Stew

Serving: Serves 8 | Prep: | Cook: |Ready in:

Ingredients

- 2 tablespoons Olive Oil
- 2 cups Onion Chopped
- 2 cups Carrots Sliced
- 1 1/2 cups celery sliced
- 1 tablespoon dried dill weed
- 4 cups assorted mushrooms sliced
- 6 cups Vegetable broth
- 1 teaspoon Salt
- 1 teaspoon Black Pepper
- 2 tablespoons Low sodium Soy sauce
- 1/2 cup Parsley, minced
- 1 1/2 cups whole grain brown rice pasta

Direction

- 1. In a 4 quart soup pot, heat Olive oil over medium-high heat. Sauté the onion and carrots for a few minutes and add celery and dill weed. When browned add mushrooms and cook lightly. Add broth, salt, pepper and Soy Sauce. Bring to boil, reduce heat and simmer 30 minutes.
- 2. Return to boil and add parsley and pasta. Boil 2 minutes and turn off heat. Allow to stand 10 minutes while pasta continues to cook. Serve.

139.   Walnut Crusted Halibut

Serving: Serves 6 | Prep: | Cook: |Ready in:

Ingredients

- Walnut Crusted Halibut
- 6 (6-8oz) halibut fillets, skin removed
- 1/2 teaspoon kosher salt
- 1/4 teaspoon freshly ground black pepper
- 1½ cups panko (Japanese breadcrumbs)
- 1 cup chopped walnuts
- 1/2 cup freshly grated Parmesan
- 2 tablespoons melted butter
- 1 tablespoon horseradish
- 1 tablespoon Dijon mustard
- 1 tablespoon chopped fresh flat-leaf parsley
- 1 tablespoon chopped fresh dill
- 1 teaspoon lemon zest
- 1 tablespoon olive oil
- Lemon Wine Sauce
- 1 teaspoon olive oil
- 2 tablespoons finely chopped shallots
- 1 cup dry white wine
- 2 tablespoons fresh lemon juice
- 2 tablespoons butter
- kosher salt and freshly ground black pepper

Direction

- Preheat oven to 425°F. Line a baking sheet with aluminum foil and coat with non-stick cooking spray.
- Pat the fish dry with paper towel and season with salt and pepper. Place on prepared baking sheet 1/2 inch apart.
- For the crust, in a medium bowl, combine panko, walnuts and Parmesan. Mix in melted butter, horseradish, Dijon mustard, parsley, dill and lemon zest to form a crumbly mixture. Divide panko mixture evenly atop fish and press gently to adhere. Drizzle 1 tbsp. olive oil on top of fish. Bake until cooked through, 12-15 minutes.
- For the sauce, in a medium saucepan, heat 1 tsp olive oil over medium heat. Add shallots and stir for 2 minutes, until slightly softened.

Turn heat to high and add white wine and lemon juice. Boil until liquid is reduced, about 6-8 minutes. Reduce heat to low and stir in 2 tbsp. butter until melted. Remove from heat and add fresh dill. Season with salt and pepper to taste. Serve over crusted halibut.

140. Warm Bread Salad With Smoked Salmon, Roasted Vegetables & Creamy Dill Dressing

Serving: Serves 4 | Prep: | Cook: | Ready in:

Ingredients

- For the dressing:
- 1 tablespoon Champagne vinegar
- 4 tablespoons crème fraîche (or Greek yogurt)
- 2 tablespoons dill, chopped finely
- salt and freshly ground pepper, to taste
- 3 tablespoons extra-virgin olive oil
- For the salad:
- 6 slices of rustic bread
- extra-virgin olive oil, for coating bread and vegetables
- 1 pound zucchini (about 2 to 3 zucchinis), stemmed and sliced in half lengthwise
- 2 cups cherry tomatoes (about 1 pint)
- 8 large green onions, sliced in half lengthwise
- sea salt, to taste
- 8 ounces hot smoked salmon, broken into bite-sized cubes
- dill, for garnish

Direction

- For the dressing:
- In a small bowl, whisk together the vinegar, crème fraîche, dill, salt, and pepper until incorporated. Slowly whisk in olive oil. Set aside.
- For the salad:
- Preheat your oven to 325° F (or bring a grill to medium-high heat). Brush the bread with a thin coating of olive oil and cut it into bite-sized cubes. Spread the bread out on a baking sheet and bake on the middle rack of the oven for 15 to 20 minutes, or until golden and crisp on the edges. Remove crisped bread and set aside. (The bread should feel like croutons in crispness, though you can certainly adjust to accommodate your tastes if you prefer a softer, soggier bread salad.)
- Increase the heat of your oven (or grill) to 450° F.
- Brush the zucchini, tomatoes, and onions with a thin coating of olive oil. Spread the zucchini on a baking sheet and, on a separate baking sheet, the tomatoes and green onions on a wire rack. Sprinkle all the vegetables with sea salt. Place the green onions and tomatoes in the upper third of your preheated oven and the zucchini in the lower third of your oven. Occasionally nudge the tomatoes and onions as you cook them. Remove the green onions when they turn slightly golden and the bases are tender, about 7 minutes, and set aside on a cutting board. Remove the cherry tomatoes once you notice nearly all of their skins have broken open, about 12 to 14 minutes. Place the cherry tomatoes in a large bowl (the bowl you plan to serve the salad in) and set aside. Finally, remove the zucchini once it is cooked through, tender, and the edges have browned slightly, about 15 minutes. Add the zucchini to the cutting board with the onions.
- While you're waiting for the vegetables to cool, rewarm the bread in the oven at 450° F for 2 to 3 minutes.
- Once cool enough to handle, slice the zucchini into roughly uniform 1/2-inch pieces and add to the bowl with the tomatoes. Slice the green onions into 1-inch long pieces and add to the bowl. Add the salmon and bread and use your hands to massage all of the ingredients with 3 to 4 tablespoons of the dressing. Add a little bit of the dressing at a time until it reaches your desired consistency.
- Garnish with fresh dill and serve immediately.

141. Warm Lentil Salad With Goats Cheese, Cherry Tomatoes And Walnuts

Serving: Serves 4 | Prep: | Cook: | Ready in:

Ingredients

- For the Salad
- 1 cup Uncooked brown lentils
- 1/4 teaspoon coriander seeds
- 1/4 teaspoon cumin seeds
- 1 splash Olive oil
- 1 smalll hot red chilli, deseeded and finely chopped
- 2 small cloves of garlic, finely chopped or grated
- 1/2 red onion thinly sliced into half rings
- 2 cups vegetables eg pumpkin, sweet potato, snow peas, peppers
- 5 ounces cherry tomatoes, halved
- 2.5 ounces soft goats cheese
- 1/2 can chick peas, draiend and rinsed
- 1/2 cup walnuts, roughly chopped
- 1 handful fresh dill, roughly chopped
- For the dressing
- 1 teaspoon apple cider vinegar
- 1 1/2 teaspoons lemon juice
- 1/2 teaspoon walnut or olive oil
- 1/2 teaspoon salt

Direction

- In a large bowl, soak the lentils in at least twice the amount of water for at least 6 hours or overnight. Drain and rinse them and place them in a saucepan (hold on to the bowl as you'll be needing it) with at least twice the amount of water and 1/2 tsp salt. Boil for 15-20 min or until cooked through (but not mushy!).
- Preheat the oven to 180C. If using diced pumpkin or sweet potato, toss these in a drizzle of olive oil and a generous pinch of salt, and spread out on a baking tray. Place in the oven until just cooked through (20 mins for sweet potato, 10-15 mins for pumpkin). At the same time, place walnuts on a baking tray in the oven for 8-10 mins or until slightly browned. Remove and allow to cool.
- In a large non-stick fry pan, dry roast the cumin and coriander seeds until fragrant. Powder in a mortar or pestle or a spice grinder. In the same fry pan, heat 1 tbsp. olive oil and add powdered cumin and coriander seeds. Allow to sizzle for a minute or so, then add chili and garlic. When garlic is browned, add onion and other vegetables (apart from pumpkin, sweet potato and tomatoes). Fry over medium heat for 3-5 mins until the vegetables are slightly browned but still crisp.
- In a small bowl or clean, empty jar, mix together the dressing ingredients until the salt has dissolved as much as possible.
- Now it all comes together! In the same large bowl that you used to soak the lentils, toss together the lentils, cherry tomatoes, saucepan mixture, sweet potato or pumpkin (if using), chick peas, dill and dressing. Taste and add more salt if needed. Serve warm topped with walnuts and chunks of goats cheese.

142. Whisky Cured Salmon

Serving: Serves about 8 people | Prep: | Cook: | Ready in:

Ingredients

- 1 two-pound wild salmon filet, boned, skin on
- 1 cup coarse sea salt
- 1/2 cup dark brown sugar
- 2 tablespoons black peppercorns, crushed
- 2 tablespoons juniper berries, crushed
- 1/2 cup of your favorite whisky
- 2 bunches dill

Direction

- Line a baking sheet with plastic wrap and set aside.
- Rinse the salmon under cold running water and pat dry with paper towels.
- In a bowl, mix together the salt, sugar, peppercorns, and juniper berries. Sprinkle half the salt mixture onto the prepared baking sheet and spread one bunch of dill on top.
- Lay the salmon skin-side down on the dill and drizzle with the whiskey. Cover with the remaining dill, and top with the rest of the salt mixture.
- Tightly wrap the salmon with plastic wrap and weigh down with a cast iron pan or tin cans. Refrigerate the salmon for 48 hours, turning the fish over halfway through.
- When ready to serve, remove the plastic wrap from the salmon. Using the back of a knife scrape the cure mixture off the fish and lay on a large wooden board. To serve, thinly slice the salmon into diagonal strips leaving the skin behind. The fish can be stored in the fridge for 5 days.

143. Whole Wheat Crusted Chicken Pot Pie With Kale, Butternut Squash, And Fresh Herbs

Serving: Serves 4 to 6 | Prep: 0hours0mins | Cook: 0hours30mins | Ready in:

Ingredients

- For the crust:
- 1/2 cup all-purpose flour
- 1/2 cup plus 1 tablespoon whole wheat flour
- 1/2 teaspoon salt
- 1/2 teaspoon sugar
- 1 tablespoon finely chopped parsley
- 1 teaspoon finely chopped thyme, leaves only
- 1 teaspoon finely chopped dill
- 4 tablespoons cold butter, diced
- 4 tablespoons cold vegetable shortening
- 5 tablespoons ice water
- For the pot pie:
- 1 whole raw chicken, or 2 large raw chicken breasts
- 3 cups chicken stock, up to 4 cups
- 6 ounces chopped bacon or pancetta, up to 8 ounces
- 1 bunch kale, or hearty green of choice
- 2 cups diced butternut squash, or yams
- 1 cup green peas (if frozen, no need to thaw)
- 1 medium onion, finely chopped
- 4 large garlic cloves, chopped or thinly sliced
- 1 small serrano pepper (or 1/4 teaspoon hot pepper flakes)
- 1 tablespoon chopped fresh sage
- 1/2 tablespoon chopped fresh thyme leaves
- 1/4 cup all-purpose flour
- 2 tablespoons half-and-half or heavy cream
- 1 egg, beaten with 1 teaspoon of water
- 1 pinch kosher salt and freshly ground black pepper to taste

Direction

- If using a whole raw chicken: Break the chicken up, reserving the thighs and wings for another meal. Remove the skin from the breasts and discard the skin. If making a stock from the carcass, cover the breasts and refrigerate. If not making stock, skip to step 3.
- If making stock: In a large pot, add the chicken carcass, 1 quartered onion, 1 carrot cut into thirds, 2 ribs celery cut into thirds, 1 head of garlic cut in half crosswise, 1 bay leaf, some parsley and thyme sprigs (or any herbs you have lying around like dill or cilantro), 1/2 tablespoon whole black peppercorns. Feel free to add other leftover veggies like a chopped leek, parsnip or turnip, or even a Parmesan cheese rind. Let's clean out that fridge! Bring to a boil and simmer for 3 to 4 hours (or longer), occasionally skimming the top. Carefully strain the broth and return broth to the pot. Discard solids.
- Make the crust: In a large bowl, sift the flours, salt, and sugar. Stir in the chopped parsley, thyme, and dill. Cut in the cold butter and

shortening using a pastry cutter or food processor and mix until mixture looks grainy, with pea-sized pieces. Add cold water, starting with 4 tablespoons. Fluff and mix gently with a fork. If the dough feels too dry, add more water as needed. I usually don't need more than 6 tablespoons. Gather into a ball, flatten a bit, wrap in plastic and chill for at least an hour.
- Preheat oven to 425° F. Place rack in the middle position.
- Add the chicken breasts into the pot with the stock, bring to a boil, lower heat to low, and simmer, covered, for 10 to 15 minutes, depending on the thickness of the breasts. Chicken should be opaque-looking and cooked through. Remove chicken, let it cool enough to handle, and shred by hand. Keep this stock — you'll be using it later!
- In a large pan or Dutch oven, cook the bacon or pancetta over medium heat for 5 minutes, stirring often, until crispy. Remove with a slotted spoon and add to the shredded chicken. Leave the rendered fat in the pan; you need about 1 tablespoon. (Add olive oil if needed.)
- Chop the onion, garlic cloves, and serrano pepper. Add to the pan with the bacon fat and sweat over medium-low heat for 5 to 7 minutes until onion is translucent. Add half of the chopped sage and thyme and cook another minute.
- Meanwhile, chop the kale (make sure to remove tough stems) and add to the pan. Cook the kale until wilted, about 3 minutes. Season the veggies with some kosher salt and fresh pepper (a couple of pinches of each).
- Stir in the flour and cook another minute. Now add the stock, one cup at a time, stirring well as you go. The flour will thicken it.
- Add the diced squash to the pan. The squash should be barely covered with the stock, so add a bit more if necessary. Partially cover the pot and cook on medium low until squash is tender, about 8 minutes. In the last 2 minutes of cooking, add the sweet peas and the rest of the herbs. At the end of cooking, stir in the half-and-half or heavy cream.
- Turn off heat, add the bacon and shredded chicken to the pot and stir to combine. Season with more salt and pepper to taste.
- Transfer the potpie filling to a large, deep pie dish or a gratin dish. (Alternatively, you can cook this in a large, deep, ovenproof cast iron skillet and add the crust right to the skillet, but you'll have to move the leftovers to store them in the fridge).
- On a lightly floured surface, roll out the dough and place on top of the filling. Cut off excess dough around the edges and pinch the dough around the edges to seal. Cut a few decorative slits on top; these will let steam escape. Brush the crust with the egg wash.
- Cook in the preheated 425° F oven until crust is golden and slightly brown in places, about 30 minutes. Rotate pie half way through so it cooks evenly.
- Let the potpie rest at least 10 minutes before serving, preferably 15 to 20.
- Enjoy this delicious, comforting potpie and relish in knowing that you just cleaned out your fridge. :)

144. Yellow Split Pea Soup With Dill & Edamame

Serving: Serves 4 | Prep: | Cook: |Ready in:

Ingredients

- 1 tablespoon olive oil
- 1 medium onion, chopped
- 2 medium carrots, chopped
- 2 stalks celery, diced
- Pinch salt
- 2 cloves garlic, minced
- 1 cup yellow split peas
- 4 cups vegetable broth
- 2 tablespoons fresh dill, minced
- freshly ground black pepper

- salt to taste
- 1 cup frozen, shelled edamame beans, thawed
- Pinch smoked salt, optional

Direction

- Heat the oil in a medium size soup pot over high heat. Add the onion, carrots, celery and a pinch of salt. Reduce the heat to medium and sauté until the vegetables start to get tender, about 5 minutes. Add the garlic and sauté 1 minute longer.
- Sort and wash the peas. Add to the pot along with the broth, dill and pepper. Bring the soup to a boil; reduce the heat to low and simmer, partially covered, until the peas are tender, about 45 minutes, stirring occasionally. You may need to add water if the soup gets too thick. Check for seasoning.
- Stir in the edamame beans and simmer for an additional 5 minutes. Ladle the soup into bowls and sprinkle with a bit of the smoked salt.

145. Yemenite Chicken Soup

Serving: Serves 6-8 | Prep: | Cook: | Ready in:

Ingredients

- The Soup
- 1 chicken, 3-4 lbs., cut into 8 pieces
- 2 large onions
- 8 garlic cloves, peeled
- 1 large tomato, quartered but not cut all the way through
- 2 stalks celery
- 3 carrots, peeled and cut into 1/4 inch rounds
- 3 potatoes, peeled and cut into 1/2 inch cubes
- 1/4 bunch parsley, finely chopped
- 1/4 bunch dill, finely chopped
- 1/4 bunch cilantro, finely chopped
- 2 tablespoons salt, or to taste
- 2 tablespoons hawayij (see spice ingredients below)
- 2 tablespoons z'hug (see spice ingredients below)
- 1/3 cup hilbe (see spice ingredients below)
- The Spices
- 2 tablespoons black peppercorns (for hawayij)
- 1 tablespoon black caraway seeds (for hawayij)
- 1 teaspoon cumin seeds (for hawayij)
- 1 teaspoon coriander seeds (for hawayij)
- 1 teaspoon cardamom seeds (for hawayij)
- 2 teaspoons turmeric (for hawayij)
- 1 pinch saffron (optional) (for hawayij)
- 4 green serrano or jalapeno peppers, stems removed and seeds removed but reserved (for z'hug)
- 1 whole head of garlic (for z'hug)
- 1/2 bunch fresh cilantro, rinsed and dried (for z'hug)
- 1/2 bunch fresh parsley, rinsed and dried (for z'hug)
- 2 green cardamom pods, peeled (for z'hug)
- 1 teaspoon cumin (for z'hug)
- 1 teaspoon salt (for z'hug)
- 1/2 cup olive oil (for z'hug)
- 3 tablespoons fenugreek powder (for hilbe)
- 1/2 cup water (for hilbe)
- juice of 1/2 lemon (for hilbe)
- 1 teaspoon salt (for hilbe)
- 1 teaspoon z'hug (see recipe above) (for hilbe)

Direction

- First, 1-2 hours before you begin cooking the soup, start soaking the fenugreek powder to make the hilbe (see spice ingredients).
- Then start making the soup: Put chicken in a large pot and cover with water by three inches. Bring to a boil, skimming off scum, and let it boil for 30 minutes.
- While soup is boiling, make the hawayij: To make hawayij, pound peppercorns, caraway seeds, cumin seeds, coriander seeds, cardamom seeds, turmeric, and (optional) saffron using a mortar and pestle, or use a small food processor.
- After soup has been boiling for 30 minutes, add onions, garlic, tomato, celery, salt, and

hawayij. Simmer for another hour, until chicken is tender.

- While soup is simmering, make the z'hug: Put peppers, garlic, cilantro, parsley, cumin, cardamom, and salt in a food processor. Begin processing and gradually add 1/4 cup olive oil, then puree. Adjust for seasonings, adding pepper seeds if you want more heat. Remove contents to a glass container and cover with olive oil. (This will keep for months in a refrigerator in an airtight jar.)
- Now, make the hilbe: The fenugreek seeds should soak in water for at least 3 hours, until the mixture is gelatinous. Add z'hug, lemon juice, and salt, then beat until smooth using an electric hand mixer or whisk. Adjust seasonings. It should be very spicy.
- After the soup has been simmering for an hour, add carrots, potatoes, and all but two tablespoons of the parsley, dill, and cilantro. Cook until vegetables are cooked through.
- Stir in z'hug and hilbe, and serve as is, or over rice. Sprinkle remaining herbs on top.

146. Zesty Cucumber Yogurt Dip

Serving: Makes 2 cups | Prep: | Cook: | Ready in:

Ingredients

- Zest from one lemon
- 1 Cucumber
- 12 ounces Greek yogurt
- 3 tablespoons finely chopped fresh dill
- Coarse sea salt to taste
- 1 slice of lemon and 1 sprig of dill for garnish

Direction

- Peel and cut the cucumber in half lengthwise. Scrape out the seeds with a spoon. Slice the cucumber halves into very thin half-moons.
- Mix all ingredients in a bowl and chill for at least two hours. Garnish with a slice of lemon and a sprig of dill. Serve with pita chips.

147. Zucchini Cupcakes With Lemon Dill Frosting

Serving: Makes 12 cupcakes | Prep: 0hours20mins | Cook: 0hours20mins | Ready in:

Ingredients

- Cupcakes
- 3/4 cup plus 2 tablespoons (175 grams) sugar
- 2 large eggs
- 1/4 teaspoon salt
- 1 medium-large lemon
- 3/4 cup plus 2 tablespoons (132 grams) white rice flour
- 1/3 cup plus 1 tablespoon (40 grams) oat flour
- 1/2 teaspoon baking soda
- 1 teaspoon baking powder
- 1/2 ground cinnamon
- rounded 1/4 teaspoons lightly packed, freshly grated nutmeg
- 1 1/2 cups (170 grams) lightly packed, coarsely grated zucchini (I use large holes on my box grater)
- 3 tablespoons (9 grams) finely chopped fresh dill leaves including only the thinnest tender bits of stem
- 1/4 cup plus 2 tablespoons (80 grams) extra-virgin olive oil
- Frosting
- 1/2 cup (15 grams) lightly packed fresh dill leaves with very thinnest tender bits of stem
- 4 cups (225 grams) powdered sugar
- 1 stick (113 grams/4 ounces) unsalted butter, slightly softened
- 1 medium-large lemon
- 1 tablespoon extra-virgin olive oil (see note)
- 1 Equipment:
- 1 Cupcake pan with 12 cavities
- 1 Stand mixer with paddle attachment

Direction

- Position a rack in the lower third of the oven and preheat the oven to 350°F. Line the pan with paper liners.
- To make the cupcakes, grate the zest of the lemon in the bowl of an electric mixer fitted with the paddle attachment (or in a mixing bowl if using a handheld mixer). Add the sugar, eggs, and salt. Beat at medium-high speed until the mixture is thickened and lighter in color, about 2 minutes. Or beat with a handheld mixer on medium-high speed for 3 to 4 minutes.
- Add the rice and oat flours, baking soda, baking powder, cinnamon, nutmeg, zucchini, and dill and beat on low speed just until blended. Beat in the olive oil. Divide the batter evenly among the cups.
- Bake until a toothpick inserted in the center of cupcakes comes out clean and dry, 18 to 20 minutes. Set pan on a rack to cool for a few minutes before tipping cakes out onto the rack to cool completely before icing or storing.
- To make the frosting, put the dill into the bowl of a food processor fitted with the steel blade. Add 5 or 6 tablespoons of the powdered sugar and process until the dill is pureed, scraping the sides of the bowl as necessary, and adding a little more sugar as necessary until the mixture is a thick syrupy puree. Grate the zest of the lemon directly into the processor bowl and add the remaining sugar and the butter in chunks. Process until smooth and spreadable. Process until completely smooth and spreadable, scraping down the sides of the bowl as necessary. Add the olive oil and pulse to blend.
- Note: I always try to sneak in a little more extra-virgin olive oil—it adds a lovely dimension and complexity to the frosting that ties into the cupcakes—but at some point, too much oil will curdle the frosting. If that happens to you, smooth out the frosting by pulsing in a bit more powdered sugar.

148. Zucchini Soup With Feta And Fresh Dill

Serving: Serves 2 | Prep: | Cook: | Ready in:

Ingredients

- 2 large zucchini squash
- 1/2 cup onion, diced
- 4 springs fresh dill, chopped
- 4 tablespoons feta, crumbled
- 2 tablespoons olive oil
- salt and pepper to taste

Direction

- Heat the olive oil in a saucepan, on medium-high heat. Add the diced onions and cook for 3 minutes, then add zucchini and dill, and cook for another 3 minutes.
- Add 2 cups of water and 1 tsp of salt, lower to simmer and cover with a lid. Let simmer on low heat for about 30 minutes (you may need to add some more water, although the zucchini will probably release some while they cook).
- When the zucchini are very tender, remove from heat and blend with an immersion blender. You may add some more water if the soup seems too thick, or boil it for some more minutes if it seems to thin.
- Divide the soup into 2 bowls, and top each bowl with 2 tbsp. of crumbled feta. Sprinkle with freshly ground black pepper and drizzle with some olive oil. You may also add some more fresh dill on top, if you like.

149. Beet Leaf Bundles

Serving: Serves 25 | Prep: | Cook: | Ready in:

Ingredients

- 6-8 cups quinoa prepared by pkg instructions

- 2 large onions diced medium
- 1/2 pound bacon diced and browned then set aside
- 4-6 garlic cloves mashed into a paste ....this dish cannot have too much garlic so if you love garlic add more
- biggest pile of beet leaves you've ever think you will ever need...but add more cause you will need lots
- fresh dill about four cups torn up left in sprigs.....not chopped up
- 1 quart whipping cream
- celery salt, to taste
- salt and pepper
- splash well maybe a glug...of lea and perrins
- couple handfuls of panko
- 1 egg, beaten

Direction

- Preheat oven to 350 prepare quinoa as per package direction. We might have used vegetable broth but really don't recall for sure. Set aside to cool. Separate the beets from the leaves and set the stems aside. So three piles - beets, leaves and then the stems
- Steam stems ...add water to the stems in a container micro safe and long enough to accommodate the stems. Steam just long enough so the stems will bend easy without breaking...but not mushy or overdone.
- While quinoa is cooling (we used a rice cooker and used a little less liquid than package directions) chop onions and add them to large bowl with quinoa. Add garlic and spices panko and egg and the cooked bacon chopped up. Mix everything up the only ingredients remaining should be the sprigs of dill, cream, leaves, stems...and the mixture should reek of garlic
- Before the bundles are assembled open some wine and pour big glasses for the group of assemblers
- You will need a glass lasagna pan or cake pan with high sides ....the largest one you have
- Either use an ice cream scoop a cookie scoop or a tablespoon for the filling to transfer to the leaves. Whatever works depending on size of the leaves. But do not make large bundles, about two bites size give or take
- Spread out the leaf (some will need to be cut to a manageable size) on a cutting board and place about 1/4 cup of mixture in the middle of the leaf and fold the corners in then place a stem flat next to the bundle...transfer the stuffed leaf folded side down on top of the middle of the stem and use stem to tie up the bundle. Transfer this tied up bundle to glass pan. Don't doddle this step must be done quickly so it stays intact. Layer them up and pile the bundles in. There will prob be about 80-100 of them. Compress them when you think there's enough. Try to keep bundles from breaking. You will run out of stems before the leaves...don't worry they should all be compacted to ensure the bundles stay intact
- Pour cream generously over them and compress again keep adding cream so the bundles appear swimming in cream....very well coated. Don't overfill pan as the cream will just boil out all over your oven.
- Add the sprigs of dill over the bundles once the cream has been added and compress the whole thing down before covering with foil
- This went in the oven when the turkey was done. With just one oven, when the bird was done it was deboned and the meat was put into one of those aluminum foil dispisable roaster pans. And then a container of turkey broth was poured over the meat, it was sealed up with sheet of foil and kept warm in the BBQ out of the way on the patio. The moisted and best bird you will ever eat...just ensure the flame is low or only one burner is on if your BBQ has multiple burners....after all the work it would be a shame to burn the turkey now at this late stage
- The beet leaf bundles, were put into the oven for about an hour and the yam casserole was added to oven the loaded mashed and anything else on the menu. Just cook the bundles first so they cook up while preparing everything else. You might want to put the

- glass container on a sheet pan to prevent oven mess and flare up
- It's time consuming but soooo worth it. This addition to our thanksgiving menu got raves and everyone was very depressed when it was all gone

150. Tomates Farcies: Vegetarian & Beef Stuffed Tomatoes, Bonus QUINOA Salad

Serving: Serves 6-8 | Prep: | Cook: | Ready in:

Ingredients

- vegetarian stuffed tomatoes
- 1 cup cooked quinoa
- 1 fennel bulb, finely minced
- 2-3 scallions, finely sliced (or chopped chives)
- 1 small bunch flat leaf parsley, finely chopped
- 1 small bunch chopped fresh dill
- 6-8 ripe roma tomatoes, emptied (inside juices and softer pulp set aside)
- sea salt & freshly ground pepper to taste
- 1-2 tablespoons extra virgin olive oil
- french style tomates farcies with grass fed beef
- 1 pound grass fed lean ground beef
- 1 yellow onion, finely minced
- 1-2 garlic cloves, finely minced
- 8 large ripe tomatoes (heirlooms are good)
- 1 large bunch flat leaf parsley, finely chopped
- Handful thyme sprigs (leaves)
- 1 small bunch fresh basil leaves
- 3 tablespoons good quality bread crumbs
- 2 tablespoons extra virgin olive oil
- sea salt & fresh ground pepper to taste

Direction

- Vegetarian stuffed tomatoes
- 1. Combine the cooked quinoa with all of the chopped herbs, green onions, very finely chopped fennel, sea salt, pepper, and olive oil. Finely chop up the tomato pulp that was set aside (from emptying the tomatoes earlier) and add to the mixture without too much of the juice.
- 2. Carefully fill the tomatoes with the mixture, put the lids on loosely, and drizzle lightly with olive oil. Bake in a 350 degree oven for 30 minutes. ** You can also add 2 tbsp. of good quality parmesan cheese to the mixture you fill the tomatoes with for additional flavor**
- 3. Fresh QUINOA SALAD with fennel: after filling the tomatoes, you should have some mixture left over. Add to this the lime juice, baby tomatoes, fennel greens, more chopped dill, and a dash of extra virgin olive oil. Serve as a quinoa salad!
- French style tomatoes farcies with grass fed beef
- 1. Cut the tops off the tomatoes, then carefully empty the insides with the help of a small paring knife and a small spoon (be careful not to pierce them). Save the softer pulp and juices from the insides in a bowl. Allow the empty tomatoes to drain, and keep their lids near them.
- 2. In a heavy pot heat 1 tbsp. olive oil, sauté the minced garlic and onions in the oil until softened and golden, then add and brown the beef with sea salt & pepper to taste. Break up the beef pieces with a wooden spoon or spatula. Chop up about 1/2 of the tomato pulp and add it with some of the juices to the browned beef and cook until the liquid is absorbed. Turn off the heat, let the mixture cool slightly, then add all of the finely chopped herbs and mix well.
- 3. Add about 3 tbsp. of good quality bread crumbs and combine well. Taste for salt, and adjust.
- 4. With a spoon carefully fill the tomatoes with the mixture all the way to the top and cover loosely with their lids. Place tomatoes tightly in a baking dish, drizzle lightly with olive oil, and bake in a 350 degree oven for about 40-45 minutes-up to an hour.

Index

A

Ale 60,72,73

Allspice 75

Almond 4,49,62,70

Apple 3,4,9,28,62,68

Asparagus 3,4,10,60,62

Aubergine 3,34

Avocado 3,10,11

B

Bacon 3,12

Bagel 3,13

Baked beans 77

Baking 46,69

Barley 4,48

Basil 46

Beans 3,4,17,29,77

Beef 3,4,5,12,36,53,92

Black pepper 43,76

Blini 3,16

Bread 3,5,10,64,84

Brisket 4,53

Broccoli 4,63

Brown rice 60

Buckwheat 16

Burger 3,4,37,50,77

Butter 3,4,5,13,17,25,33,41,61,66,78,86

C

Cabbage 3,4,20,25,53

Cake 3,23,30

Carrot 3,4,5,16,17,18,26,30,54,60,72,82,83

Cashew 3,31

Cauliflower 4,61

Celery 3,4,21,26,40,52,73

Champ 31,84

Chard 4,12,58

Cheddar 12,50,53

Cheese 3,4,5,12,13,16,31,34,42,50,56,67,69,85

Cherry 5,71,85

Chicken 3,4,5,8,18,19,20,26,42,61,64,75,81,86,87,88

Chickpea 3,4,33,34,46,72,77,78

Chips 3,18

Chives 4,52,57,67

Cider 3,20,28,62

Cinnamon 29

Cloves 27,29,54,69,75

Cocktail 56

Coconut 66

Coleslaw 4,77

Coriander 27

Couscous 4,66,67

Crab 3,11,23

Cream 3,4,5,8,13,19,20,24,26,40,61,64,68,71,73,78,84

Crumble 8,26,30,67

Cucumber 3,4,5,22,24,26,27,28,42,43,45,48,55,56,64,78,89

Cumin 27

Curry 71

D

Date 4,72

Dijon mustard 24,31,33,39,52,53,77,83

Dill 1,3,4,5,6,8,9,12,16,17,19,20,22,23,24,25,26,27,28,29,32,38,42,43,52,53,55,58,59,60,62,64,66,67,68,69,71,76,77,84,87,89,90

Dumplings 3,7

E

Edam 5,87

Egg 3,26,29,35,55,64,69

F

Fat 4,47,69

Fennel 3,4,21,27,52,55,56,65

Feta 4,5,24,66,67,69,90

Fish 3,4,25,30,45

Flour 26,64,70

G

Garlic 29,54,62,67,69,71,75

Gin 3,17

Grapes 77

Gratin 3,15

H

Halibut 5,45,83

Ham 3,33

Harissa 49,50

Heart 3,6

Herbs 4,5,46,58,86

Herring 3,38

Horseradish 3,39,68

Hummus 3,39

J

Jam 81

Jus 48,91

K

Kale 4,5,41,42,86

Ketchup 12

Kidney 29

L

Lamb 4,43,44

Leek 3,4,20,79

Lemon 3,4,5,33,34,35,41,45,46,50,52,62,66,70,71,75,76,83,89

Lettuce 4,12,42

Lime 4,65

Lovage 4,60

M

Manchego 26

Mayonnaise 7

Meat 81

Milk 26,70

Mince 50

Mint 76

Mortadella 3,15

Mozzarella 12

Mushroom 3,4,5,13,37,48,50,52,63,67,80,83

Mussels 4,76

Mustard 42

O

Oil 3,14,22,26,29,55,62,64,66,67,69,71,83

Olive 4,26,29,46,47,49,55,59,62,65,66,67,69,71,75,76,83,85

Onion 3,12,24,29,41,43,62,69,71,76,83

Oregano 32

P

Pancakes 3,17

Paprika 3,14,22,29

Parmesan 19,25,83,86

Parsley 66,69,76,83

Pasta 4,68

Pear 3,4,41,67

Peas 3,27,41,71

Pecorino 41

Peel 24,26,28,30,42,45,47,68,74,80,89

Pepper 4,28,29,32,37,42,44,62,64,66,67,69,71,74,75,83

Pickle 3,4,12,26,27,38,42,54,55,56,58,78

Pie 3,4,5,8,25,52,70,71,86

Pizza 3,12,13,34

Plum 81

Polenta 4,77

Pomegranate 66

Pork 55

Port 3,37,64,67

Potato 3,4,5,9,14,22,26,27,28,35,47,52,62,63,82

Puff pastry 81

Pulse 10,32,40

Q

Quinoa 3,4,34,55,70

R

Radish 4,52,56

Rice 3,4,13,27,29,55,59,70

Ricotta 64

S

Salad 3,4,5,6,8,9,21,24,26,27,29,31,33,34,35,38,41,42,47,52,55,56,62,63,64,65,67,68,71,79,84,85,92

Salmon 3,4,5,6,10,11,14,16,22,23,26,44,63,66,67,68,70,82,84,85

Salt 4,6,8,11,16,19,27,28,29,32,36,37,40,42,43,45,49,56,60,61,62,63,64,66,67,69,75,76,83

Sardine 4,64

Sausage 55

Savory 4,80

Scallop 3,15

Sea salt 21,46,79

Seafood 4,51,65

Sesame seeds 81

Shallot 64

Soup 3,4,5,18,22,26,28,35,40,46,48,58,60,61,63,72,76,80,81,82,87,88,90

Soy sauce 75,83

Spices 4,58,88

Spinach 4,63,69,70

Squash 4,5,49,72,86

Stew 3,5,14,41,77,83

Stuffing 76

Sugar 42,66,75

T

Tahini 33,34,39

Thyme 4,45,66

Tofu 71

Tomato 3,4,5,12,27,29,32,59,71,74,85,92

Trout 4,68

V

Vegan 3,5,33,83

Vegetable oil 40

Vegetables 4,5,42,43,79,84

Vegetarian 5,92

Vinegar 4,24,28,42,62,63,64

W

Walnut 5,83,85

Whisky 5,85

Wine 24,43,83

Worcestershire sauce 13

Z

Zest 5,6,15,37,68,79,89

L

lasagna 91

Conclusion

Thank you again for downloading this book!

I hope you enjoyed reading about my book!

If you enjoyed this book, please take the time to share your thoughts and post a review on Amazon. It'd be greatly appreciated!

Write me an honest review about the book – I truly value your opinion and thoughts and I will incorporate them into my next book, which is already underway.

Thank you!

If you have any questions, **feel free to contact at:** author@sauterecipes.com

Erin Williams

sauterecipes.com

Made in the USA
Las Vegas, NV
26 December 2023